ANSWER GUY

Brendan O'Connor, Neil Fine, and Gary Belsky

ESPN BOOKS

New York

Book Design by Kathie Scrobanovich

ISBN: 0-7868-8756-7

First Edition
10 9 8 7 6 5 4 3 2

Photo credits:
Getty Images: 19 top, 29 left, 41 middle, 43 top, 45, 47 top and bottom right, 49 bottom left, 51 bottom, 53 top, 55, 57 top, 61 bottom, 71 bottom, 75, 77 left and bottom, 83, 85 bottom, 87, 89, 91 top, 93, 97, 99, 101 bottom, 103, 105, 109, 111, 113 bottom, 115, 117 bottom, 119, 121, 127, 129 top, 131, 133 bottom, 135 top, 139 top, 143 bottom, 145 bottom, 147 bottom, 149 top, 153 top, 155

Corbis: 9 top, 15 bottom left and right, 17 top, 21 top, 23, 25 bottom left and right, 31, 32 top, 33, 34 bottom left, 57 bottom, 59 bottom, 61 top, 81, 95 bottom, 101 top, 137 top, 143 top, 145 top, 151 top

Photodisc: 9 bottom left and right, 11, 15 top, 17 bottom, 19 bottom, 21 bottom, 25 top, 27, 29 right, 32 bottom, 35 top right, 39, 41 top and bottom, 43 bottom, 47 bottom left, 49 top and bottom right, 51 top and middle, 53 bottom, 59 top, 63, 71 top, 73, 77 right, 79 top, 85 top, 91 bottom, 95 top, 129 bottom, 133 top, 135 middle and bottom, 137 bottom, 139 bottom, 141, 147 top, 149 bottom, 151 bottom, 153 bottom

Photofest: Peanuts 13, Albert Einstein 34, Abbott and Costello 35, Small World 79, Underdog 107, Humphrey Bogart 113, Three Stooges 117, Ben-Hur 122

John Broder: Bulldog 137

(Illustrations): Title page, Acknowledgments, 2, 7, 37, 69, 121, 123, 125, 162

TO | Encyclopedia Brown
Wink Martindale
Columbo
Abigail Van Buren
Inspector Clouseau
Nellie Bly
Scooby-Doo and those meddling kids
The Shell Answer Man
The Wise Son (the Wicked one, too)
The Oracle (at Delphi)
The Mirror (on the wall)

ACKNOWLEDGMENTS ⊙

There are many people to thank for their help with this book, but we're no fools—we'll start with the ones who sign our checks. John Papanek, editor-in-chief of *ESPN The Magazine*, has always been a fan of Answer Guy, as have executive editors Gary Hoenig and Steve Wulf. Michael Rooney, late of *The Magazine* and now senior vice president and general manager of ESPN Outdoors, has a really long title so he must be important. Thanks, Mike!

Dan Patrick, ESPN front man, has collaborated with Answer Guy without complaint, which is more than we can say. He even wrote the foreword for this book. To fully explain senior editor John Hassan's role in this book and in our lives would take many years. Managing editor Lynn Crimando was dogged in her efforts to seal the deal with our publisher. Speaking of which: Gretchen Young, senior editor at Hyperion, believes in Answer Guy almost as much as she believes in synergy. We're in her debt —and that of her able assistant, Natalie Kaire, as well.

The Magazine's Kathie Scrobanovich is responsible for the design of this book. She was inspired, no doubt, by Peter Yates, her boss and the finest design director to ever come out of Staten Island. Or Australia. Brenna Britton found the photos we needed.

Any factual mistakes in these pages should be blamed on us or on a conspiracy of high-level government officials (that would be our bet). Just don't blame it on our research department, led by Craig Winston and Roger Jackson and assisted by John Boell.

A while back, Dave Eggers and Zev Borow (late of *Might* magazine) brought Answer Guy in from the cold streets of San Francisco. They introduced him to us when they came east. We owe them.

Finally, a special thanks to all the people we've quizzed, cajoled, confounded, and misquoted. They are the true Answer Guys.

CONTENTS ▼ ANSWER GUY

⊙ SECTION II: TOOLS OF THE TRADE

⊙ SECTION III: WORD

⊙ SECTION IV: CUSTOM MADE

⊙ INDEX

FOREWORD ⊙

When I got the call to write this foreword, I was a bit surprised.

"Dan, this is Answer Guy."

"Yeah, right."

Not that Answer Guy hasn't reached out to me before. We've worked together on a couple of occasions, having tackled the slippery slopes of "winning and losing" and "clutch" for *The Magazine*. We help each other out all the time. I give him numbers (Barry Sanders, The Answer, P. Diddy). He gives me numbers (Tennis Hall of Fame, U.S. Orienteering Federation, Larry King). We do the same thing, after all. We find Truth. And then we pass it on.

But what surprised me was that he *called*. AG's usual M.O. is the fax, the e-mail, or the message relayed by third party. I never get a friendly ring because AG is almost always on the phone doing his job. Just ask the folks in Cooperstown, Canton, and Springfield. He's got no time for chitchat.

So, yeah, at first I was skeptical. But he established his identity and here I am. One thing that did not surprise me was his voice. Clear, commanding, crisp, AG's voice rings with an authority that a marine drill instructor would envy. Think John Facenda with a dash of James Earl Jones. No wonder people tell him what he wants to know. The power of that voice compels you. I gave up my SAT scores before he even asked for them.

We all know that the world of sports contains many mysteries. Rooting them out requires diligence, creativity, and persistence. My colleague Answer Guy has all these qualities. This tome is the result of a lot of hard work by a man more than suited to the task.

Enjoy and learn.

Dan Patrick
Bristol, Connecticut
Spring 2002

ANSWER GUY UNCOVERED

Where the stones of ignorance are
turned over with the shovel of
knowledge.

Who is Answer Guy?

*Neil Fine, Answer Guy's boss at ESPN
The Magazine:* We're not at liberty to
say. **Says who?** No comment. **But ...**
And don't quote me. **Hmmm.** *Alan
Grant, Answer Guy's cantankerous
coworker:* Tell me, Guy, why is it
windy in March? **I have no idea.**
Show me the guy who can answer
that, and I'll show you the Answer
Guy. **That's not sports, Al.** Tough.
*Gary Belsky, Answer Guy's handler
at The Magazine:* I can tell you that
I've never met anyone quite like
him. **What's he like?** Answer Guy is
the most intelligent, resourceful,
kindhearted, handsome person I
know. If he were a woman I'd ...
[*Ed.'s note: Our apologies. Sometimes
Answer Guy hears what he wants. Let's
try that again.*] *Belsky:* All I can say
is that Answer Guy is very good at
what he does. **And what does he do?**
He asks the tough questions, gets the
tough answers, and fills up the rest
of the space with as much triviata
as possible. It's informative and
entertaining. **Infotainerting?** Could
be. **How did he learn his craft?**
Nobody knows. **C'mon, nobody?** *Zev
Borow, freelance writer and friend
of Answer Guy:* There's a rumor that

The question
at hand.

A source,
always in
italic.

What a
source has
to say,
always in
Roman.

Answer Guy
speaks, always
in boldface.

A word from
Answer Guy's
sponsors (his
editors).

Where the sharp point of a column is often hinted at bluntly by a parallel metaphoric construction.

Sister Immaculata, like some of Answer Guy's sources, has changed jobs since appearing in the column.

he was once a Micronesian strongman with bad skin and very good taste, but I don't think it's true. **Why not? Look at his complexion, nary a blemish!** *Emily, Answer Guy's wife:* Oh, he's got an answer for everything all right—a regular know-it-all. **You're too kind. Has he always been so smart?** [*Ed.: Cue harp, fuzzy lens.*] *Sister Immaculata, Answer Guy's third-grade teacher:* When was the war of 1812? **I don't know.** *Sister Immaculata and her entire class of evil third graders:* Ha-ha. **Never *(sniff)* again!** [*Ed.: End flashback.*] *Dave Eggers, raconteur and childhood mentor of Answer Guy:* He never really got over that grade-school humiliation. He's been obsessed with finding the answers to obvious questions ever since. **What a guy. But do you know who he is?** He's you, you goof. **How do you know?** The little drawing, that's you to a T. ◄

This is The End.

ANSWER GUYESE ⊙

Someday, when *The Magazine* is delivered telepathically, you won't need any help to understand what Answer Guy is talking about—you'll be one with him. Until then, here's a helpful guide. Frankly, it's not much of a substitute.

ALAS— A term of woe, generally uttered in the face of the cold realization that all knowledge is illusory and, in the end, when it comes right down to it, the only answer to most of these questions—and to most of the questions we ask ourselves as we stare into the abyss at the heart of the universe—is: "Nobody knows." At least not for sure.

ATTACK!— Answer Guy likes to say this at the slightest provocation, a symptom of his willingness to fight for the cause.*

AYE— Means yes, especially in matters nautical and Scottish.

BRING IT ON!— When it comes to the struggle for knowledge, AG is nothing if not ready to mix it up.

DARN TOOTIN'—This means that the speaker spoke truth. The expression undoubtedly has something to do with horn blowing. What that might be is for someone else's book. *See also*: Word.

DISH IT— Like "Hit me" [see below], but not.

GRRRR— Like a tiger, bear, or monkey—and certain kinds of fish. Meant to convey savage enthusiasm.

HA!— Connotes genuine astonishment colored by a knowing bemusement at the absurdity of it all.

HIT ME— Blackjack talk for "I want another card," but Answer Guy talk for "I want another tidbit of sublime erudition."

HEY, YEAH!— Exclaimed when somebody points out something interesting that old AG hadn't thought of.

OKAY THEN— Indicates that Answer Guy is satisfied with the source's previous statement. *Compare*: *Oo*-kay then.

OO-KAY THEN — Indicates that Answer Guy may or may not be satisfied with the source's previous statement, but is satisfied that the source has gone a little wacky on him.

SO I'M TOLD — The typical response when one source says something another has already said.

'TIS — Irish for "It is," as in, "'Tis true what you say about the general state of things in the field of animal husbandry." *Antonym*: 'Tisn't

VRAIMENT? — French for "really?" and a prime example of Answer Guy's penchant for speaking in a foreign language. Not that he's actually fluent in any of them.

WAY AHEAD OF YA — Somebody just said something covered in a previous column, which may or may not be previous in the book since we didn't do this chronologically, which is why we give you page numbers.

WORD — Emphatic agreement with the speaker's previous statement or point of view, delivered in an understated and retro-hip way. *See also*: Darn tootin'.

YEESH — Blech.

YIPE! — Meant to convey fear. Should be read in a high-pitched voice, like Bugs Bunny in the one when he and Daffy find the cave full of treasure and Daffy rubs the lamp and the genie comes out and Daffy stuffs him back in with his webbed feet, yelling, "No, no, no! Mine, mine, mine!" and the genie comes back out and says, "You have desecrated the spirit of the lamp. Prepare to face the consequences," and Bugs says, "Yipe!" and Daffy says, "Consequences, shmonsequences, so long as I'm rich." And then the genie zaps him.

YOU'RE TELLING ME — Someone is wasting Answer Guy's time with stuff he already knows, as if he'd be called Answer Guy if he didn't already know.

*Causes may vary.

RULES TO PLAY BY

▶ Section 1

Where the cats of chaos are returned to the bag of order—with no chance for parole.

Why is a basket worth two points?

Marty Blake, NBA scouting director: Back when America was first settled, the Pilgrims decided it would be better if a basket was worth two points. **Really?** No, not really. That's just my way of saying I have no idea. **Next time try, "I have no idea."** Well, you know, basketball was invented because it was too damn cold in the winter to do anything outside. The YMCA [*Ed.'s note: in Springfield, Mass.*] had to come up with something to keep people from dropping their membership. **Steal the Bacon wasn't cuttin' it?** Exactly. Try Doug Stark at the Hall of Fame. He won't know either, but don't tell him I said so. I'm still politicking for induction. **Already called him. He's out until Monday.** How about Mike Soltys at ESPN? He definitely won't know. *Mike Soltys, PR guy, ESPN:* I don't know. **Hey, Marty got one right!** *Harvey Pollack, director of statistical information, Philadelphia 76ers:* It goes back to Dr. Naismith. I've never known it to be any other way, and I've been here since Day One. **Before the Pilgrims?** In 1946, I was in PR with the Philadelphia Warriors. They say Red Auerbach goes back that far, too. But he's retired. He lives in Texas. **Oo-kay then.** *Bill*

Himmelman, NBA historian: They had to differentiate a field goal from a foul shot. In some very early leagues—around 1902—a field goal was one point and a foul shot a half point. That didn't last. People don't like fractions. **Why?** They're unwieldy. **Oh. But why differentiate field goals from free throws?** It was a rougher game, with tackling and grabbing. **Like the Knicks.** Right. Getting a basket was a lot harder. **Like the Cavs.** Right. A free throw is easier. It shouldn't be worth as much. **Like a Bulls ticket.** Right.

Where the soft-speaking Rough Riders of accuracy charge up the hill of error—carrying very big sticks.

Why do teams get four chances to make a first down?

Kent Stephens, curator, College Football Hall of Fame: Early on, you got three chances to go five yards. **Easy!** No, boring. Offenses would just gang-rush the line and try to trample over the opposition. **Charge!** It was quite dangerous. In 1905, 18 people were killed playing college football. **Heavens!** There was a big push to ban the game. **Sacrilege!** They had to do something to curb the violence. **Boooo!** In 1906, Teddy Roosevelt called a conference of university presidents—Harvard, Yale, and Princeton. **Brains!** They decided that the game should be more wide-open and wanted to discourage the so-called mass-momentum style of play. First, they legalized the forward pass. **Attack!** Then, they increased the yardage from five to ten. **First down!** With more ground to cover, teams had to be more creative. They couldn't just ram into each other all the time. **Prudence!** But ten yards was a long way to go in three downs. So, in 1912, they added a fourth down, hoping that would help increase scoring. **Touchdown!** *John Gable, Ph.D., executive director, Theodore Roosevelt Association:* Roosevelt fanatically believed in football. He felt it called forth qualities of hearty-

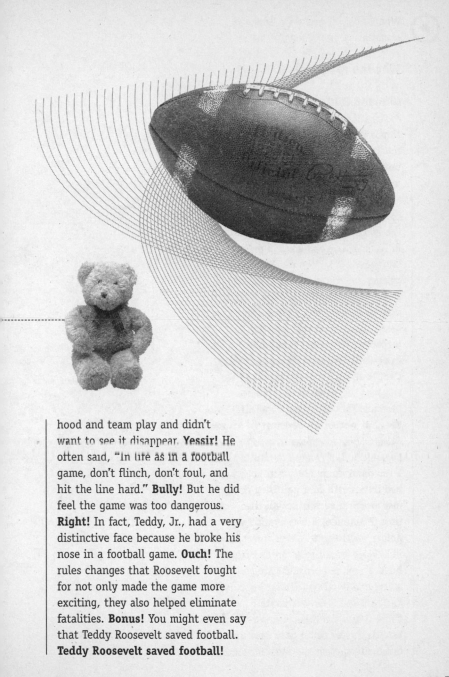

hood and team play and didn't want to see it disappear. **Yessir!** He often said, "In life as in a football game, don't flinch, don't foul, and hit the line hard." **Bully!** But he did feel the game was too dangerous. **Right!** In fact, Teddy, Jr., had a very distinctive face because he broke his nose in a football game. **Ouch!** The rules changes that Roosevelt fought for not only made the game more exciting, they also helped eliminate fatalities. **Bonus!** You might even say that Teddy Roosevelt saved football. **Teddy Roosevelt saved football!**

Where doubt's dirty refrigerator is scoured—even the meat drawer!

Why the extra point?

George Stewart, 49ers special teams coordinator: I don't have a clue. Maybe it's a bonus for scoring a touchdown. **Well, naturally, George, but ...** Hey, if you get the answer, let me know. **You'll be the first.** *Mike Stock, Redskins special teams coach:* I don't have the answer. But you know, the kicking game is really important in Canada. The end zone is much larger and ... [*Ed.'s note: Portions deleted due to irrelevance.*] *Wayne Sevier, Chargers special teams coach:* It used to be a dropkick. **You don't say.** Yeah, then, when they started to placekick, they built a mound to kick from—a little two-inch mound of dirt. **Cool. But why the extra point?** Well, think of the name of the game— football. That tells you something. **Yes, but not what we want to know.** *Saleem Choudhry, researcher, Pro Football Hall of Fame:* I'm looking at a rule book from 1884. A touchdown was only worth four points, a field goal worth five. **But ... why the extra point?** Actually, it was worth two points ... **Uh-huh ...** Well, football did evolve from rugby. **So did rugby have an extra point?** *Ed Hagerty, editor and publisher, Rugby Magazine:* Yes. Still does. **Why is that?** I think it was the other way around. **What was the other way around?** Originally, and this is speculation, a

try [*Ed.: Rugby's version of a TD.*]
wasn't worth jack. It just gave you
an opportunity to *try* to kick a goal,
which was worth one point. **So the
extra point was once the only
point?** Right. But over time, the
emphasis shifted and scoring a try
became more valuable. **And the kick
just sort of hung around?** Probably.
Gotta call George back. *Stewart:*
Thanks, but I already found out.
You did? Yeah, I called Jack Clark,
the rugby coach at Cal. **Well, you
could have called us.** I tried, but I
got your machine.

Where the little lost mittens of naughty little kittens are found and attached to their sleeves.

Why are there 18 holes in a round of golf?

Ken Baron, senior editor, Golf & Travel Magazine: That's a good one. **Thanks.** I used to have a book that explained it. But if I were you, I'd just make it up. **Like what?** Like the Legend of the Young Squires. **Squires?** Yeah, young Scottish laddies. They were allotted a certain number of balls. When they ran out, the round was over. **That doesn't work on so many levels. But thanks anyway.** *Nicolas Shump, member services consultant, Golf Course Superintendents Association of America:* Ask David Bishop. He knows all that stuff. He's always giving us little quizzes. **Sounds like a jerk.** No, he's my boss. **Okay then ...** *David Bishop, director of information services, GCSAA:* Well, there's fact and there's lore. The fact is it comes from St. Andrews in Scotland. **And the lore?** They say a bottle of scotch contained 18 jiggers. When the bottle was empty, the round was over. **I hear ya, pallie.** *Barry Kerr, managing director, Heritage Golf of St. Andrews, Scotland:* I can shed a little light on that. **Do.** The early golf courses had no fixed number of holes. Some were 5, some 12, some 20. At the R&A [*Ed.'s note: Royal and Ancient Golf Club of St. Andrews.*], we had 11 holes that

went straight along the water. They'd play 11 out, turn around, and play the same 11 back. **Hey, I get it—a "round" of golf!** Right. In any event, a round was 22 holes. **That's a lot of jiggers.** Right. At some point [*Ed.: Oct. 4, 1764.*], they decided that the first four holes were too easy, so they made them into two. That made nine holes out, nine back. **18!** Right. **Still enough to irk the wives, though.** Right.

Where the cookies of confusion are dunked in the whole milk of clarity.

Why is the Kentucky Derby only open to three-year-olds?

Cathy Schenck, librarian, Keeneland Racetrack, Lexington, Ky.: All I know is it was patterned after the English Derby, which is run by three-year-olds. Try Epsom Downs in England. *Jonathan Spence, PR rep, Epsom Downs:* Well, basically, two-year-olds are still too young. But when they're three, fillies run in the 1,000 Guineas, colts in the 2,000 Guineas. Those are like qualifiers for the Darby. **The Darby?** Right. **What's a Darby?** Oh right, you chaps say derby. **Isn't that how it's spelled?** Well, yes. But it's a man's name. The Earl of Derby. **Darby?** Exactly. *Alan Shuback, Brit, foreign racing editor, Daily Racing Form:* The idea developed in England around 1776 when Colonel Anthony St. Leger held a race at Doncaster for three-year-olds. It was called the St. Leger Stakes. Then in 1779, General John Burgoyne—who, incidentally, lost the crucial Battle of Saratoga in the Revolutionary War and who was keenly interested in horse racing—developed the Epsom Oaks, a mile-and-a-half race for fillies. **I'm with ya.** He called it the Oaks because that was the name of his house in Epsom. **Oh.** The next year, several nobles, including the Earl of Derby, General Burgoyne, and the playwright Richard Brinsley Sheridan, ran colts in the

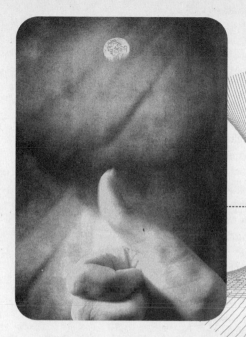

first English Derby at Epsom Downs.
Darby? Exactly. *Tony Terry, director
of publicity, Churchill Downs:* When
the Kentucky Derby started in
1875, most of the best stallions and
broodmares had been seized by the
Civil War armies. Colonel M. Lewis
Clark, who founded Churchill Downs,
wanted to showcase the Kentucky
breeding industry. A three-year-old
Derby winner would be very valuable.
Longer life at stud. **So they're not
the best horses, just the luckiest?** I
suppose. Do you know why it's called
a Derby in the first place? **Nope.**
The Earl of Derby and Sir Charles
Bunbury flipped a coin. **You mean
it was almost the Kentucky
Bunbury?** Exactly.

Where attention-starved queries get some TLC, a trip to the zoo, and ice cream after!

Why is the 24-second clock 24 seconds?

Marty Blake, NBA director of scouting: It was Danny Biasone's idea. Danny revolutionized basketball. He should really be in the Hall of Fame. **Yeah, yeah, so should Shoeless Joe. Who is Danny Biasone?** He owned the Syracuse Nationals in the '50s. Before the shot clock, games would be like 4-2 at halftime. We'd be reading newspapers on the sidelines. **4-2 at halftime?** *Harvey Pollack, director of statistical information, Philadelphia 76ers:* The problem really wasn't until the fourth quarter. The team with the lead would just hold the ball until time ran out. You'd have to foul them to get it back. **But why 24 seconds?** *Bill Himmelman, NBA historian:* It's kind of like folklore that gets passed down. **Like Mikey and the Pop Rocks?** Who? **Forget it.** Biasone is considered the father of the shot clock. The story goes that he took the average number of possessions in a game and divided that into 48 minutes. It worked out to about 24 seconds per shot. It's really not very scientific. **Well, it's better than nothing. But it does beg the question of why 48 minutes?** The game had always been 40 minutes. I guess you'd have to credit Naismith with that. So when the BAA merged

with the NBL to form the NBA in 1949 … **Easy with the initials there, Bill.** Sorry. Anyway, they wanted to elevate the pro game above the amateur game. Like how college baseball is seven innings and the pros play nine. [*Ed.'s note: Actually, they play nine in college, too, but you get the idea.*] They probably chose 48 since it's so easily divided by four. **But so is 60. You know, like football and hockey.** True, but to go from 40 to 60 would have been too drastic. Don't forget, football has the running clock, so you stand around for five or six minutes doing nothing. **Kinda like your typical Heat-Grizzlies game.**

Licking the Tootsie Pop of confusion to reveal a chewy chocolate center of clarity.

Why do we run the bases counterclockwise?

Paul Dickson, author, The New Dickson Baseball Dictionary: There's a Finnish game where they run backward. And in cricket they run front to back. Then there's rounders. [*Ed.'s note: An old British game involving a stick, a ball, and four posts.*] Call Dave Kelly. *Dave Kelly, sports specialist, Library of Congress:* Check a *Spalding Guide.* Do you have one? **Uh, sure.** There's one from 1886 that has the early rules of baseball. **The *1886* edition? We might not have that handy.** Well, you need to find out why rounders runs counterclockwise. *Shirley Walker, chairman, National Rounders Association, Nottingham, England:* I don't know, I'm afraid. **How far back does rounders go, anyway?** Well, I gather it goes back to Elizabethan times. **Then it's the queen's fault. Every silly custom goes back to the queen.** Also, I suppose it's more natural to go to the right after hitting. **Then how do you explain baseball below the equator, where they run clockwise?** Like water going down the plughole? **Like water going down the plughole.** *Michael Fuller, secretary, St. Kilda Baseball Club, Melbourne, Australia:* We don't run the bases clockwise, actually. **Any idea why**

you run them counterclockwise?
My guess is it has to do with the
Coriolis effect. **Oh, you mean
the force that explains why the
movement of air or water is
directed clockwise in the northern
hemisphere and counterclockwise
in the southern?** That's the one.
**Well, that's fine for you guys, but
why don't we run from third to
first?** No idea.

Where the hordes of cluelessness are baptized in the waters of illumination.

Why is a perfect game 300 points?

Mark Miller, public relations, American Bowling Congress: You're only knocking down 120 pins, so they needed some kind of point system to get to 300. **Why?** Well, you get ten points for knocking down all the pins. Then you get bonus points. **Why?** If you throw a spare, you get bonus points equal to the number of pins you knock down on your next ball. For a strike, you add the next two balls. **But isn't knocking down all the pins the point of the game?** Yeah. **So why do you get bonus points for doing what you're supposed to do?** Well, that's just how you score. **You realize how silly it is, right?** It goes back a couple of hundred years. **I see.** *Travis Boley, curator, International Bowling Museum and Hall of Fame:* Through most of the nineteenth century, everywhere you'd go the game was scored differently. **Madness!** Thomas Curtis came up with the 300-point scoring system around 1895. **Why?** He's widely regarded as the father of tenpin bowling. I guess 300 just made sense. **To whom?** To him. **Oh.** And if you think about it, ten pins, ten frames, the game really calls for a good round number. **Sure it does—100.** You know, modern tenpin bowling originated as a religious

ceremony. **Hallelujah!** Around
A.D. 300, Saint Boniface was trying
to convert the German hordes to
Christianity, and he adopted some
of their customs. **Bright boy.** The
Germans walked around with these
sticks, called "*kegels*," which they'd
throw at littler sticks called *heides*.
Those wacky Germans. Boniface
imbued this ritual with religious
significance by making the *heides*
represent demons. Knocking them
down showed your purity of spirit.
**Cool. And how many points was
that worth?**

Where secret ingredients of the Cosmic Soup are revealed, gratis.

Why do baseball games have nine innings?

Bill Francis, researcher, Baseball Hall of Fame: Before the Civil War, baseball was in its rudimentary stages, with different towns playing by different rules. **Madness!** The most common version was played to 21. **Like Ping-Pong?** Right. Each team got an equal number of "hands," or chances to bat, and the first to score 21 runs—called "aces"—won. **Cool.** But there was no limit to the number of hands, so some games would last forever, while others would be over quickly. **Like a Royals game?** Right. In 1858, the National Association of Base-Ball Players held a convention to codify the rules. There was a push for seven innings, but they eventually settled on nine. **Any idea why?** Not really. *John Thorn, coeditor, Total Baseball:* The person most responsible for the nine-inning game is Lewis F. Wadsworth. He played first base for the New York Knickerbockers in the 1850s, and at a team meeting, he put forth the nine-inning idea. **Why?** One theory says it was in keeping with the number of players on the field, but at the time, there were anywhere from eight to eleven players per side. Wadsworth also appears to be responsible for the dimensions of the diamond. **But didn't that Cartwright guy come up with that**

earlier? Well, some people think that the main innovations credited to Alexander Cartwright—90 feet between bases, nine men per side, nine innings—didn't come about until long after he'd gone to California in search of gold. **Ah, the irony. Sure are a lot of nines, though.** *Edgardo Torrelvoma Numerology Center, New York City:* Nine is the number of supreme intelligence. **Yes. Yes.** It represents completion and victory. **I see. I see.** What's your birthday? **6-1-70.** You're going to make a lot of money. **Hot dog!** You also help people. **How very true.**

Where the minutemen of cogency fire upon the redcoats of nonsense.

What's the story behind the scoring system in tennis?

Joanne Sirman, communications department, International Tennis Federation, England: We have a booklet on this. Would you like me to send you one? **Can't you just tell me?** It's quite complicated. I can't sum it all up in one sentence. **How about a hint?** Let me send you a fax. **You don't actually know the answer, do you?** Yes, I do. Right here in this little book. It's really quite useful. **Sure, if you bother to read it.** Now look here, I don't have time to explain all this over the telephone. Do you want me to fax you or not? **Yes, please.** *Linda Barrett, media department, French Tennis Federation, France:* Bonjour. **Parlez-vous anglais?** Yes, I do. **Bon. Quelles sont les origines de la methode de marquer les points en tennis?** Oh my goodness gracious. **Qu'est-ce qu'il y a?** We get this question all the time. **Vraiment?** I think we have it in an old book somewhere. Can you hold? **Mais oui!** [*Ed.'s note: 10 minutes later.*] Sorry, I can't find it. **Zut alors!** *Mark Young, librarian, International Tennis Hall of Fame, USA:* No one knows for sure. Some form of tennis has been played since the twelfth century. **Mon Dieu!** Excuse me? **Skip it.** One theory says it comes from an old French coin, the 60 *sou*. Tennis was played for stakes.

The *sou* could be broken into four pieces, so each point was worth one quarter of the coin, or 15. **Then why 40?** We think that's just a shortened version of 45. **But of course. And deuce?** Also French, *a deux*, meaning "two to win." **Cool. So what's "love" got to do with it?** Oh, that's the easiest one of all. **Would that it were, Mark. Would that it were.** No, really, think about it: A zero written down is kind of oval shaped. **Yeah?** The French would say *"l'oeuf,"* which means "egg." The English thought they were saying "love." Simple as that. ***Incroyable!***

Where slaves of doubt are liberated by locusts of fact. With a little push from the slaying of the firstborn.

Why do pitchers pitch off a mound?

Bill Francis, researcher, Baseball Hall of Fame: Answer Guy? **That's me.** Where ya been, Guy? You never call anymore. **The road to truth is a winding one.** It's one of the few mysteries in baseball, you know. **How flattering.** No, not you. The mound thing. **Oh. Right.** There's no reference to a height to pitch from until 1903. But we know the mound existed before then. **And how do we know that?** Because they don't explain it. **Could you explain that?** In 1903, they simply refer to it as "the mound," as if people would already know what they're talking about. **Ah.** Some people think the mound was put in to improve water drainage. But you should talk to Tom Shieber. He knows all that stuff. *Tom Shieber, Webmaster, Baseball Hall of Fame:* Nobody knows. **I was told you knew.** I don't. **Well, what** *do* **you know?** In the 1850s, they had a pitcher's line, no more than 15 paces from home. **Paces?** About a yard each. In 1863, they added a back line, creating a pitcher's box. **Cool.** You could throw from anywhere within the box, so long as both feet were on the ground when you delivered the ball. **Right. Now, about the mound.** Of course, they had to pitch underhanded. **Off**

the mound? In the 1880s, they moved the pitcher's box back, hoping to increase offense. **Yeah, but was there a mound?** In 1884, they removed all restrictions on delivery, which again hurt the hitters. **Neat, but ...** In 1893 ... **what ...** they moved ... **about ...** the pitcher to ... **the ...** 60' 6" ... **mound?** They also introduced the rubber. **Are you listening to me, Tom?** Some people say that a surveyor misread ... **Hello? Tom? ...** the blueprint notation of 60' 0" as 60' 6". **Tom!** But it's not true. **TOM!** Yeah? **The MOUND?!?** Oh. Right. Nobody knows.

Where the cads of treachery are
vexed by the gents of virtue.

Can you steal first base?

*Eric Enders, researcher, Baseball Hall
of Fame:* No. **Why?** Rules. **What
rules?** Baseball's rules. **Oh, them.**
There are 23 legal ways to get to first.
Do tell. Walk, intentional walk, hit
by pitch, dropped third strike, failure
to deliver pitch within 20 seconds,
catcher interference, fielder
interference, spectator interference,
fan obstruction ... **Isn't that ...** fair
ball hits umpire, fair ball hits runner,
fielder obstructs runner, pinch-runner,
fielder's choice, force out at another
base ... **Aren't those ...** preceding
runner put-out allows batter to reach
first, sac bunt fails to advance runner,
sac fly dropped, runner called out on
appeal ... **Wait, which ...** error, four
illegal pitches, and if a game is
suspended with a runner on first and
that player is traded prior to the
makeup, another player can take his
place. **That's only 22.** Oh, right.
Single. *Borrring. John Thorn, coeditor,
Total Baseball:* Two players stole first,
Germany Schaefer in 1907 and Fred
Tenney around 1900, but they did
it from second. The idea was to
induce a throw so the runner on third
could score. **Tricky.** I suppose, but
it didn't work. And now it's illegal.
Pity. You know, Ned Cuthbert of the
Philadelphia Keystones invented
the stolen base in 1865. **Rapscallion.**
Baseball was primarily intended to

TIME-OUT ⊙ A Brief History of Inquiry

Emergence of Homo sapiens, but very little is questioned. (You hunt, you gather, what else do you need to know?)

In first recorded inquiry, Snake asks Eve: "Did God really tell you not to eat from any of the trees of the Garden?" Turns out to be the first recorded trick question.

Age of Buddha. Plump man wanders around spreading wisdom to a hungry people. Wisdom like: "Believe nothing."

499,999 – 3,762 B.C.   **c. 3741 B.C.**   **551 – 479 B.C.**

500,000 B.C.   **3761 B.C.**   **563 – 483 B.C.**

Mankind begins ageless search for meaning in a cold, dark universe.

In the first recorded homicide investigation, God asks Cain the whereabouts of his brother, Abel. Cain responds with the first use of the old answer-a-question-with-a-question gambit: "Am I my brother's keeper?" Doesn't work then, either.

Age of Confucius. Bearded man wanders around, proclaiming, "Knowing is not as good as loving; loving is not as good as enjoying." Apparently, he and the Buddha were in cahoots.

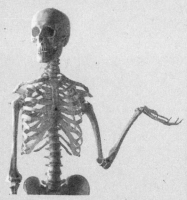

provoke mirth. **Verily.** The main amusement was not to hit lusty blows, but the exposition of spry fielding and nimble baserunning. **Huzzah!** So credit for a steal was based on pluck, like taking an extra base or stretching a single. **Good show!** It's also likely the term "stealing" wasn't equated to larceny, but was akin to "stealing away," as in taken through guile or subterfuge. **Good ol' derring-do.**

Socrates develops a scheme to draw forth knowledge by asking questions, and humbly names it after himself. Soon after, he commits suicide, thus capping a harsh couple of centuries for inquiry.

Dark Ages. People are freaked, not least by the druids, of whom it is asked, "Who are they, and what are they doing?"

Spanish Inquisition begins, kicking off centuries of painful questions to which, it turns out, there are no correct answers. On the plus side, it later inspires lavish musical number in Mel Brooks's *History of the World: Part I*.

287–212 B.C.   **800s, roughly**   **Early 1600s**

469–399 B.C.   **A.D. 477–1400**   **1478**

Greek mathematician Archimedes runs around naked screaming "Eureka! Eureka!" after discovering a method to test for pure gold. An appreciative public responds: "What the hell does 'eureka' mean, anyway?"

Punctus interrogativus— the question mark—is invented by Gregorian monks as part of a system of musical notation. Inquiry gets a calling card!

Hamlet, Shakespeare's melancholy Dane, asks: "To be, or not to be?" Answer still pending.

René Descartes postulates that the only thing that cannot be doubted is doubt itself, therefore the doubter must exist: *Cogito, ergo sum.* (Rough translation: "I think, therefore I am Answer Guy.")

Age of Enlightenment. Or so we've been told.

Sigmund Freud publishes *Interpretation of Dreams*, which, in a nutshell, says that we're all afraid to die or want to sleep with our mothers. Or both.

1664–66

1841

1905

1637–41

1700s

1900

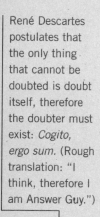

Sir Isaac Newton defines the universal law of gravitation, explaining why everything is so damn heavy.

Edgar Allan Poe pens the first detective story, "The Murders in the Rue Morgue." (An orangutan did it. Seriously. Go with "The Tell-Tale Heart.")

Albert Einstein unveils the Special Theory of Relativity, answering that long-asked question, "What does E equal?"

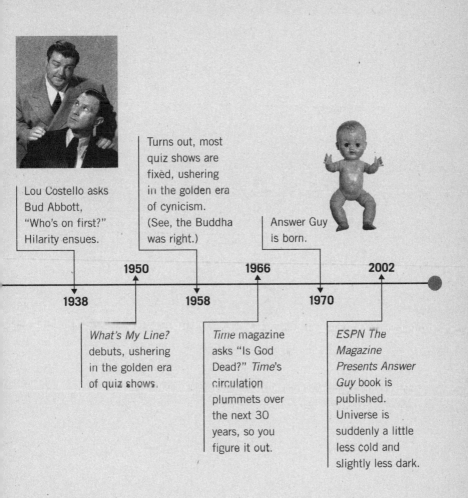

Lou Costello asks Bud Abbott, "Who's on first?" Hilarity ensues.

Turns out, most quiz shows are fixed, ushering in the golden era of cynicism. (See, the Buddha was right.)

Answer Guy is born.

1950

1938   **1958**   **1970**

1966   **2002**

What's My Line? debuts, ushering in the golden era of quiz shows.

Time magazine asks "Is God Dead?" Time's circulation plummets over the next 30 years, so you figure it out.

ESPN The Magazine Presents Answer Guy book is published. Universe is suddenly a little less cold and slightly less dark.

TOOLS OF THE TRADE

▶ Section 2

Where the ice-cream truck of fact hears the childish shrieks of conjecture, slows—then speeds on.

Why do they wave a checkered flag at the end of a car race?

Donald Davidson, historian, Indianapolis Motor Speedway: I've been working on this one for 30 years. **Any luck?** Not really. I do know that they've been using the checkered flag here since Day One. [*Ed.'s note: 1911.*] Most of the other flags have changed in meaning, like red meant a clear course and green signaled one lap to go. But the checkered flag has always marked the finish line. **Why?** From what I can tell, it comes from bicycle racing. Officials would wear checkered vests to sort of mark out the course. If the riders saw the vests, they'd know they were still on the right track. **Pretty thin for 30 years there, Don.** Best I got. The only other theory is that some French woman threw a checked scarf to an official at the end of a race, but it's not much to go on. **No, it isn't.** *Unnamed receptionist, Union Cycliste Internationale: Allo?* **Hello. Do you speak English?** *Oui.* **Is there a checkered flag in bike racing?** *Non.* **Never?** *Oui.* **Wait, "yes," there used to be, or "yes," there never was?** *Non!* **"No" as in never?** *Oui!* **I'm sorry, I'm still confused. Is there someone else ...** [*clique!*] **Oh, my.** *Peter Nye, historian, U.S. Bicycling Hall of Fame:* No one knows. **C'mon,**

no one? I've read a bazillion articles on car racing and haven't found the answer. The best I've come up with is that early engines were so loud they needed something visual to mark the finish line. **Like a sign that says "Finish Line"?** I suppose. But, you know, most of the early automakers were also bicyclemakers. **Really?** Oh, sure. Walter Chrysler, Louie Chevrolet, Albert Champion. They all came out of cycling. **Uh-huh.** You see, history is written randomly, so answers are often hard to come by. **Don't I know it, Pete. Don't I know it.**

Where the clinches of viscosity are broken by the ref of lubrication.

Why is it called a boxing ring?

Shilpa Bakre, media services director, USA Boxing: As opposed to a boxing square? **Precisely.** That's a very good question. **We aim to please.** I have absolutely no idea. **Alas.** But let me give you some phone numbers. Try the IBF. **'Kay.** *Disembodied phone company voice:* We're sorry, your call cannot be completed as dialed ... **Hmmm.** *Bakre:* Or the WBO. *Answering machine:* Hi there, this is Nick's house. If you'd... *Bakre:* How about the WBA? *Receptionist, La Asociación Mundial de Boxeo, Venezuela:* ¡Hola! AMB. **Buenos días. ¿Habla inglés?** No. **Qué pena.** *Bakre:* Try the NABF. *Sam Macias, president, North American Boxing Federation:* That's a very good question. **So I'm told.** I have no idea. **You're not alone, Sammy.** *Nigel Collins, editor-in-chief, Ring Magazine:* It's just a guess, so I wouldn't want to be quoted. **Tough.** Before they had ropes, spectators would naturally form a ring around the fighters. **Naturally.** But people were always invading the circle. They had guys with whips and clubs to beat back the crowd. **How sporting.** The ropes weren't meant to keep the boxers in so much as to keep the fans out. **Ah, bloodlust.** *Jeff Brophy, researcher, International Boxing Hall of Fame:* According to *The Encyclopedia of Boxing*, by Gilbert

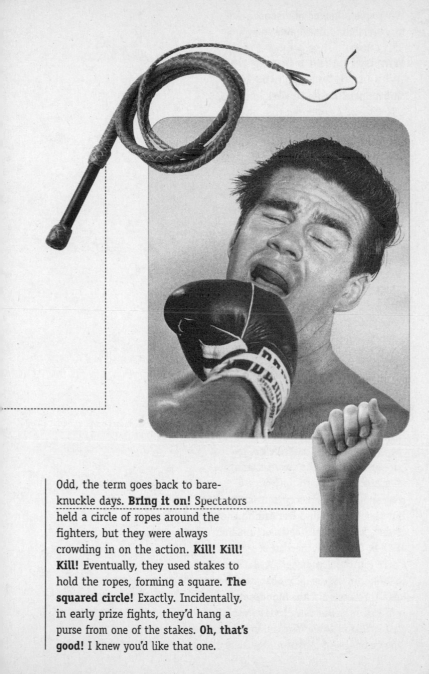

Odd, the term goes back to bare-knuckle days. **Bring it on!** Spectators held a circle of ropes around the fighters, but they were always crowding in on the action. **Kill! Kill! Kill!** Eventually, they used stakes to hold the ropes, forming a square. **The squared circle!** Exactly. Incidentally, in early prize fights, they'd hang a purse from one of the stakes. **Oh, that's good!** I knew you'd like that one.

Stuffing the box of chicanery with the ballots of forthrightness—early and often.

Why do they use chains to measure for first downs?

Tim Davey, assistant director, NFL game operations: The chain is ten yards long, whaddayathink? **But the field already has yard markers.** But the ball sometimes lands between the markers. **So all they really need is a yardstick, to measure the space between the lines.** But they have the chains. **But why?!** Listen, the linesman spots the ball, right? **Right.** Then he comes over to the sideline and puts his heel down to mark the line of scrimmage, right? **Right.** The rear stick goes there. Ten yards from that spot is a first down. **But. Why. Do. They. Need. The. Chains?** To measure the ten yards! *Sigh. Saleem Choudhry, researcher, Pro Football Hall of Fame:* You know, the chains predate the gridiron. **Aha!** As far back as 1898, the rules make reference to the linesman having two assistants, "each equipped with an iron rod connected by a stout cord or chain." **Sounds reasonable.** The gridiron didn't develop until between 1904 and 1908. So they needed the chains to measure the yardage. **Then the chains are essentially obsolete.** Not at all. You need the chains to measure a first down. **But isn't that what the gridiron is for?** Partly, yes. But the chains are definitive, they help

eliminate controversy. **But you realize this whole construct is totally arbitrary.** How so? **It's based solely on the linesman's interpretation of where to spot the ball.** Yeah? **So the perception of objectivity is illusory.** Are you okay? **Don't you see?! It's all meaningless, man!** I gotta go. *Dr. Tom McGoldrick, clinical psychologist, Brooklyn, NY:* Sometimes things that lack objective meaning take on an agreed-upon social meaning. **But what if *I* don't agree?** Then perhaps it's time to question your need for unambiguous answers. **Sorry, Doc, no can do.**

Pelting the cars of illusion with the well-packed snowballs of reality.

Why do hockey players wear shorts?

Ralph Dinger, NHL Publishing: You mean the pants? **They're shorts.** Right, short pants. You know it is rather silly, the game being played on ice and all. **Word.** But the stockings and garter belts reach to the top of the groin area. **Easy, Ralph.** And once they start skating, I imagine they heat up pretty quickly. **Yipe!** *Dan Diamond, editor, Total Hockey:* They used to wear quilted knickers. **Oh, did they?** Like football players. They wore socks to hold their shin pads. Over time, the socks got longer and the pants shorter. **I'll say.** For a while, in the '70s, some teams wore Cooperalls, kind of like padded girdles. **Sissy boys.** They wore long pants over those. **Smart move.** The rules no longer allow long pants. **Why not?** Tradition. **Gotcha.** That's pretty much all there is to it. **In that case, why are they always whacking the goalie's pads?** The pads used to be stuffed with deer hair. The hair would soak up moisture from the ice, which made the pads malleable. They'd whack them with their sticks to make them wider. **You're good.** It's nothing. **Okay, then—what's CCM stand for?** Canadian Cycle and Motor Company. **Makes sense.** Bikes don't sell well in the wintertime, so they started making hockey equipment to up

profits. **Greedy boys.** I suppose.
**By the way, stockings, garter belts,
quilted knickers? What kinda
game is this?** *Michael, Answer Guy's
peewee hockey–playing nephew:* First
of all, Uncle Answer Guy, they're not
stockings. They're socks. **Pretty long
socks there, Mike.** And I don't wear
a garter. I use tape. **Why?** Garters are
for sissy boys. **Darn tootin'!**

Plucking the pledge pin of duncehood from the uniform of scholarship.

Why do bowling shoes come in such festive colors?

Bruce Pluckhahn, American Bowling Congress Hall of Famer: Bowling goes way back. [*Ed.'s note: Egypt, 500 B.C.*] But the game as we know it began in Germany [*Ed.: A.D. 300.*], where it's called *kegel*. When the shoes came in, I can't say. **Danke, anyway.** *Jim Dressel, editor, Bowlers Journal International:* I don't know. I do know why three strikes in a row is a "turkey." **Hit me.** Bowling lanes were attached to taverns. They'd give you a turkey when you got three straight strikes. **Tasty—though tangential.** *Travis Boley, curator, International Bowling Museum and Hall of Fame:* Bowling was very much a back-alley game played behind taverns and saloons. **I get it: bowling alley!** Right. But the game became associated with gamblers and drunks ... **God bless 'em ...** and was banned for a time [*Ed.: 1840s.*] in Connecticut and New York. **Fascists! Now about those shoes.** Indoor bowling got big in the '30s, after Prohibition was repealed. **Party on!** Until then, special shoes were rare. *Jeff Lind, owner, bowling shoe–maker Linds Shoes:* My father, Leslie, was a cobbler in St. Paul, near the Hamm's brewery. One day, around 1936, Rags Ragogna, captain of the Hamm's bowling team, came into Dad's shop and asked if

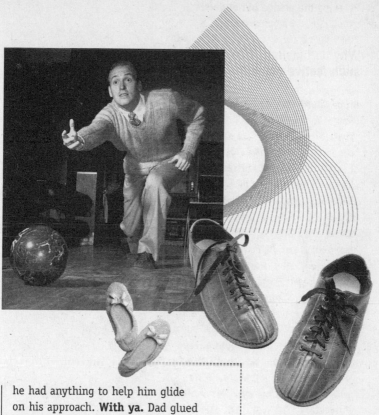

he had anything to help him glide on his approach. **With ya.** Dad glued buckskin to his soles. **Clever.** Next day, Rags brought in the rest of the team and said, "You don't know what you got here." **He didn't!** He did. Then, Dad realized he could make a better shoe starting from scratch. **Eureka!** Yup. He'd just finished a job for an Armenian dance troupe, so he used leftover red kidskin to make the bowling shoes. After Hamm's beat Stroh's a few days later, Stroh's asked Dad for red shoes, too. The rest, as they say, is history. **Pretty spiffy.** You betcha.

Where answers to the most vexing questions are uncovered like treasures from a famous sunken ship.

Why are tennis balls fuzzy?

Mark Young, historian, International Tennis Hall of Fame: I don't know that. **No idea?** No. *Lizz Marascilu, United States Tennis Association:* I don't know. **Fine. Onward!** *Laura Kurzu, director of communications, Penn Racquet Sports:* The fuzz controls the speed of the ball through the air. It also allows a player to control the ball. **How?** It has to do with torque. Actually, I don't know if "torque" is the right word ... **Sounds good to me. Torque. Hmmm.** Yes. It's used in beer bottles. **What is?** Torque. It's used to twist off the cap. I'm sure your readers know all about torque. **I'm sure they do. So what's the fuzz made out of?** Wool. **Wool? Why wool? Why not cotton? Terry cloth? Polyester?** Well, you need the fuzz that wool has. The fuzz gives you the grip. And wool is the only material that fluffs. **Fluffs?** It's like when you put a sweater in the dryer, and when it comes out, it's tighter, but fluffy. That's like what happens with animals. **In the dryer?** Right. Smaller, but very, very fluffy. **So, while I have you, why are the balls packaged like they are, all vacuumed up?** To retain the pressure at the core of the balls. It helps them last longer. **Kind of like Pringles.** Right! Like Pringles. **Laura, do you**

like Pringles? No. **I do. But back to the wool. Is it specially engineered wool?** Well, it's from New Zealand. **Is that why it smells the way it does?** Yeah, sure. But you should talk to Steve Judge at the felt plant. *Steve Judge, vice president and general manager, Tex Tech Industries, Tempe, Ariz.:* Sheep are abundant in New Zealand. We need a lot of wool. **About how much?** About a million yards a year. **And is it true the sheep of New Zealand smell like tennis balls?** Who said that? **Laura from Penn.** No, they don't. But they don't smell that great, either ...

Where the parched throat of doubt is quenched by cool, refreshing certitude.

Why does the logo appear on only one side of the Steelers helmets?

Ken Draznik, marketing manager, Riddell, Inc., official supplier of NFL helmets: I've heard two stories: Back in the '60s, when the team first started using the logo, they either ran out of decals, or they were too cheap to buy enough for both sides. **Ouch. Is that the official version?** *Ron Wahl, communications coordinator, Pittsburgh Steelers:* Well, back when they developed the logo, the team wasn't sure about using it. They wanted to test it first, see how it looked before ordering enough for both sides. **So they just put it on one side?** Right. **Couldn't they have, you know, tested it in practice or something?** No, because you don't get the full effect—11 guys on the field, in a real game, all that. **Fair enough.** And that year, the team had their best season yet, so they left the helmet that way—for luck. **Merril, is that what you've heard?** *Merril Hoge, former Steelers RB:* I know the real story, because the guy who was there told me: See, when the decals came in, there was a mistake—they were all the same. So when you put them on the right side, they were fine, but on the left side, they were backward. **Hmmm. Did you ever feel, you know,**

lopsided? Lopsided? **Yeah, playing with only one decal and all.** No, I never felt lopsided. **Is the old equipment manager still around?** Yeah. He just retired recently. *Tony Parisi, equipment manager, Steelers, 1965–1997:* It wasn't a mistake, actually. It's the logo. The logo reads left to right. You can't have it on the left side—it faces the wrong way. **Aha! And you applied the decals yourself?** Oh, yeah. But it's not easy. It's hard to put something round on something round. **That is hard.** They might look easy to put on, but they're not. **I believe you.** Now, the guy who replaced me, he can really put them on! **You don't say.** Yeah, try it sometime, see how long it takes. You'd be surprised.

Refracting the dull light of misconception through the crystalline prism of sharpness.

Why are the Browns helmets orange?

Amy, media relations office, Cleveland Browns: I'm pretty sure it's always been orange. **I see.** I don't think there's any particular reason, though. **You'd be amazed.** *Dino Lucarelli, alumni relations manager, Cleveland Browns:* That's a silly question. **To each his own.** Of course, I'm a silly guy. **You go, Dino!** Originally, the helmet was plain white. **Pure.** But in the '50s, they decided to go with orange. **Any particular reason?** They felt it would dress up the uniform, you know, make it more attractive. **Hmmm ...** [*Ed.'s note: Cue harp, fuzzy lens.*] *Answer Guy's brother Frank:* How did your date go? *Frank's friend Kevin:* Not bad. She was a bit of a Cleveland Brown, though. *Frank:* Cleveland Brown? *Kevin:* You know— great uniform, bad helmet. [*Ed.: End flashback.*] ... **no accounting for taste.** *Lucarelli:* Come to think of it, the orange helmet was first used only for night games. **Looked good in the dark, eh?** I suppose. They started using it full-time in '52. But you know, the Browns aren't called the Browns because of the color brown. **Actually, I didn't know.** It's true. Paul Brown was the coach when the team was founded in Cleveland. He was very popular with players and

fans. He didn't really like the idea, but he agreed to allow the team to be named for him. **What a guy.** They were originally going to be the Panthers. **What happened?** There was a defunct semipro team called the Panthers. They still had rights to the name. The owner wanted a piece of the action. **Fat cat.** Besides, the Panthers were never very good, and Coach Brown didn't want the new team to be associated with losing. **Ah, the irony.**

Where the neutral zone of doubt is encroached upon by the stunting linemen of assuredness.

Why do Michigan helmets have that funky design?

Jay Levin, intern, University of Michigan athletic media relations office: It's supposed to look like the head of a wolverine. Wolverines have stripes on their heads. **They do?** *Phil Myers, associate curator of mammals, University of Michigan Museum of Zoology:* Fiction and fantasy! Some wolverines have white patches, but I wouldn't call them stripes, and they certainly don't look like our football helmets. **Jay, you weasel! You've never even seen a wolverine, have you?** *Levin:* Nope. **Not surprising, considering there's never been a verified trapping of a wolverine in the state of Michigan, nor have any skeletal remains ever been found within its borders.** How do you know all that? **It's in your media guide.** Oh. Right. Anyway, the "stripes" thing is the answer we like to give because the real answer is pretty lame. **Truth, young Jay, is never lame.** Okay. All helmets used to look the same, until Princeton coach Fritz Crisler came up with the multicolored design in '35. He thought receivers would be easier to spot downfield. He brought it to Michigan in '38. **That is lame!** *Matt Ciciarelli, intern, Princeton SID's office:* The wing-style helmet was meant to resemble a tiger with its

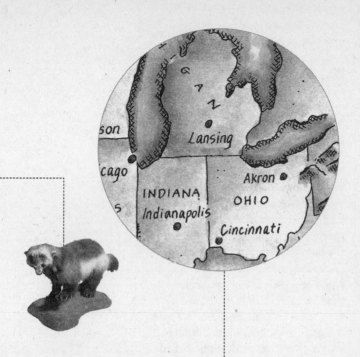

ears flared back. *Phil Myers:* Yeah, maybe after a couple of six packs. **With ya. Now about those wolverines. If there are not now nor have there ever been any wolverines in Michigan, why is it called the Wolverine State?** *Kevin, Reference and Research Center, Library of Michigan:* It comes from an 1830s border dispute with Ohio. Michiganders say the state's early settlers called themselves wolverines because of their tenacity and ferociousness. ***Grrrr!*** But Ohioans say it's because they're stupid and smell bad. **Wolverines or Michiganders?** Exactly.

Where the sand castles of indifference are swamped by the high tide of scholarship.

Why do golf courses have sand traps?

Kathryn Baker, curator, British Golf Museum, St. Andrews, Scotland: Nobody knows. **Go figure.** We do know that the earliest courses were on linksland. **Whatsland?** Linksland. You know, like links—the strip of land that links land to sea. **You mean the coast?** Not exactly. First, there's the beach, then a strip of sand and grass, then more fertile farmland. **Aye.** The middle strip, linksland, wasn't much use so it was used for grazing cattle and sheep. That's where the game developed, on the linksland. **Where there was nothing better to do.** Exactly. **Now about those sand traps?** *Gordon Moir, links manager, R&A of St. Andrews, Scotland:* You had these sand dunes, right? **Right.** The sheep would burrow down behind them to take shelter from the wind. Over time, these areas hollowed out to form the bunkers, or as you Yanks say, sand traps. **Ah, what do we know.** *Andy Mutch, museum director, USGA Golf House:* St. Andrews was a rabbit farm, and some historians contend that rabbits played an important role in the development of golf. **The wascals.** Rabbits dig holes in the finest grassy areas, which they flatten out with their big feet. Over time, those areas became putting

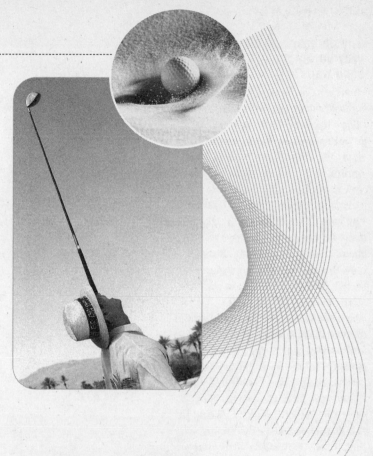

greens. **Sheep bunkers and rabbit holes? Who came up with this game?** *Glen Waggoner, golf editor, ESPN The Magazine:* The shepherds. **What shepherds?** The very bored shepherds. **What about them?** They invented the game. **Oh.** They used herding sticks to whack petrified hunks of sheep dung into the rabbit holes. It's really a very silly game. **You're telling me.**

Where truth is tattooed on the hairy back of fakery by a fat drunk.

Why do baseball players wear stirrups?

Mark Newman, senior vice president of baseball operations, New York Yankees: I don't have the slightest idea. **But all your wannabe Yanks have to wear 'em, right?** They have to wear stirrups that show six inches of blue with the opening for the sanitary sock showing two inches. **Why?** Tradition. **Like in *Fiddler on the Roof*?** No. Our guys also have to blouse their baseball pants. **Blouse? Isn't that for girls?** No. At the bottom of the pant leg there's an elastic band. Most players let that fall down. We have them turn that band under so that it kind of looks like a cuffless pair of slacks. **Classy.** But most of the players and some of the coaches don't like it. **Babies.** 'Course, when they get to the majors, they can do whatever they want. **Being in the majors rocks!** In the minors, though, we like to have little rites of initiation. **Like what else?** Nothing that we'd care to reveal. **Creepy.**
Bill Francis, researcher, Baseball Hall of Fame: Stirrups became popular around 1910. The dyes used in colored baseball socks could cause blood poisoning if a player was spiked in the shins and dye seeped into an open wound. So they added a layer of protection. **Gross.** It was a rougher game then. You've heard the stories of

Ty Cobb? **Cobb was *gay*?!** No. Later, they started making socks that were sanitary—they were manufactured in a relatively sterile environment. That's why today we call them sanitary socks. And some stirrups are even knit right into them. **So those modern stirrups are bogus?** Uh, yeah. **Man, that gets me steamed!** Well ... **What a sham.** They do look nice. **True.**

Where the neuroses of befuddlement are diagnosed by the *DSM IV* of explanation.

Why do college footballs have stripes while pro footballs do not?

Rick Walls, Eastern Region Coordinator, National Football Foundation: That's a tough one. Let me get back to you ... [*Later that day.*] Well, we found that back in 1941, the NFL did use a white football with black stripes, for night games. **And what about the striped ball used in college?** Well, one theory says it's for training, to help players see the rotation of the ball. Then again, the stripes don't even go all the way around. **So you don't really know.** No. And we don't know why the pros switched. But I'll get back to you ... [*The next day.*] I've talked to a few people, but no one seems to know. We were hoping to come up with something like someone spilling paint on the ball—something interesting—but no luck. You've thrown us a real curveball. **As opposed to a perfect spiral?** Heh, heh. Right. You might try the Hall of Fame. *Saleem Choudhry, researcher, Pro Football Hall of Fame:* I'd say it has to do with visibility, like why the pros initially used the white ball. But when NFL stadium lighting improved, the stripes became unnecessary. In college stadiums, the lighting isn't as good. **What about stripes as a training aid?** If that were true, you'd

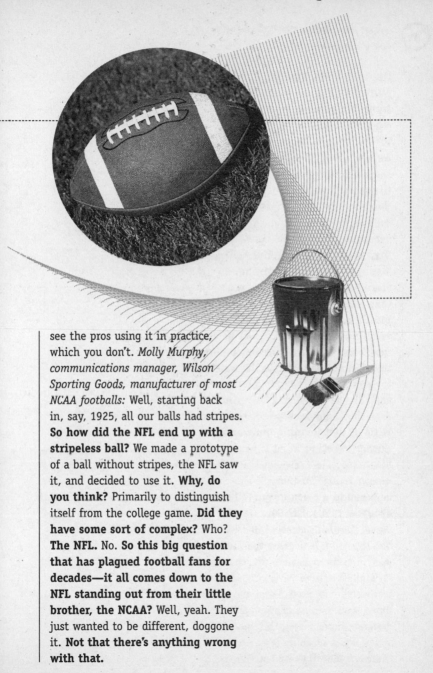

see the pros using it in practice, which you don't. *Molly Murphy, communications manager, Wilson Sporting Goods, manufacturer of most NCAA footballs:* Well, starting back in, say, 1925, all our balls had stripes. **So how did the NFL end up with a stripeless ball?** We made a prototype of a ball without stripes, the NFL saw it, and decided to use it. **Why, do you think?** Primarily to distinguish itself from the college game. **Did they have some sort of complex?** Who? **The NFL.** No. **So this big question that has plagued football fans for decades—it all comes down to the NFL standing out from their little brother, the NCAA?** Well, yeah. They just wanted to be different, doggone it. **Not that there's anything wrong with that.**

Where the amoebae of chaos evolve into the mammals of order.

Do swimmers sweat?

Larry Herr, sports science service coordinator, USA Swimming, Inc.: Yes, yes they do. **How can you tell?** We weigh them. **Why?** To see how much water they've lost. **But don't they absorb water?** What, like through osmosis? **Yeah, like a sponge.** No. **How can you tell?** It's not biologically feasible. **So why does their skin get all wrinkly?** You mean pruning? **Yeah, pruning.** No idea. **Okay, pruning aside, aren't they wet when you weigh them?** Yes. **So how do you know they're sweating?** We weigh them wet before they swim. **Why are they wet before they swim?** They jump in the water to get wet. Then they jump out and jump on the scale. Then they swim. Then they jump back on the scale. **With all that jumping, no wonder they're sweating.** Point is, without fluid replacement, swimmers lose weight during workouts. So they must be sweating. **Do you guys really care about all this stuff?** Sure we do. *Daniel Kowalski, member, Australian National Swim Team:* One year, we were in camp in Hawaii. **Ah, the struggle continues.** They did this test where one group swam and drank fluids, a second group swam and drank no fluids, and a third group swam, drank no fluids, and had thermometers stuck up their butts.

Nice. All results showed major fluid loss, extremely high temperatures, and lots of sweating. **What about pruning?** That, too. *Dr. David Friedman, dermatologist:* The dead skin, or keratin layer of the epidermis, is thick on the fingers. It swells as it hydrates, accentuating the wrinkles in the viable skin underneath. **So we *do* absorb water.** Not really, because then you could tell someone who's thirsty to take a shower. **I prefer the tub.**

TIME-OUT ⊙ Source Hall of Fame

Oddly, Answer Guy mostly *asks* questions. Then again, who'd want to be associated with someone called Question Guy? Certainly not these folks, the inaugural class of Answer Guy Hall-of-Famers.

▶ **NAME:** Saleem Choudhry
TITLE: Researcher, Pro Football Hall of Fame
AG APPEARANCES: 7
REASON FOR INDUCTION: No source gets more exasperated than Choudhry, so we owed him.
ON ANSWER GUY: "Oh jeez, another season of silly questions."

▶ **NAME:** Dan Diamond
TITLE: Editor, *Total Hockey*
AG APEARANCES: 6
REASON FOR INDUCTION: If the answer to a question is less than scintillating, Diamond comes through with other interesting filler.
GOOD TO KNOW: Diamond drives a '58 Mercedes and has a collie named Puck!

▶ **NAME:** Paul Dickson
TITLE: Author, *The New Dickson Baseball Dictionary*
AG APPEARANCES: 7
REASON FOR INDUCTION: Most of AG's baseball questions have already been asked and answered by Dickson.
ALSO WRITTEN BY DICKSON: *The Congress Dictionary*, *War Slang*, and *Sputnik: Shock of the Century*.

▶ **NAMES:** Eric Enders, Bill Francis, Rachael Kepner, Frank Vito, Tim Wiles
TITLE: Researchers, Baseball Hall of Fame
AG APPEARANCES: 11
REASON FOR INDUCTION: Access to lots and lots of books about baseball
REAL REASON FOR INDUCTION: "Is this Answer Guy? **Uh, maybe.** We *love* Answer Guy! **Oh, yeah, it's Answer Guy.**"

▶ **NAME:** Red Foley
TITLE: Official scorer, New York Yankees
AG APPEARANCES: 4
REASON FOR INDUCTION: If ol' Red doesn't know, he's not afraid to guess.
CLASSIC FOLEY: "Let's see, you got your home run, your home plate, your home on the range."

⊙ **NAME:** Nina Gilbert
TITLE: Director of Choral Activities, Lafayette College, Easton, Pa.
AG APPEARANCES: 1
REASON FOR INDUCTION: Gilbert is the official Answer Guy music historian, which makes her the only official Answer Guy anything.
FUN FACT: Gilbert put Answer Guy on her résumé. Apparently, she thinks being in the column makes her famous.

⊙ **NAME:** Alan Grant
TITLE: Retired NFL defensive back, current Answer Guy coworker
AG APPEARANCES: 3
REASON FOR INDUCTION: He sits, like, two desks away.
ON ANSWER GUY: "Whenever I ask him something—say, 'Why is it windy in March?'—he doesn't have any idea. What is that?"

⊙ **NAME:** Barry Kerr
TITLE: Managing Director, Heritage Golf of St. Andrews, Scotland
AG APPEARANCES: 3
REASON FOR INDUCTION: His colorful digressions into unrelated but nonetheless compelling subjects offered up in an amusing Scottish accent.
CONTROVERSY: Kerr, irked because he never received promised copies of *The Magazine*, is feuding with Answer Guy. Said he: "I'm not working a one-way street here, my man."

⊙ **NAME:** Steve Perrault
TITLE: Senior Editor and Director of Defining, Merriam-Webster, Inc.
AG APPEARANCES: 4
REASON FOR INDUCTION: *Hell-ooo*, his title is "Director of Defining."
JOB PERK: Perrault has authority to switch the meanings of existing words—like, say, "shoes" and "socks." (He never has. We think.)

⊙ **NAME:** John Thorn
TITLE: Coeditor, *Total Baseball*
AG APPEARANCES: 7
REASON FOR INDUCTION: John likes to talk. He's also a leading authority on nineteenth-century baseball.
ON ANSWER GUY: "I come from Nerdville, so I'm more interested in the answers to questions than in his sarcastic interpolations, which sometimes are funny, and sometimes are just smart-alecky nonsense."

TIME-OUT ⊽ Questions Better Left Unasked

Answer Guy can't sniff out everything. Or he won't, anyway. Which means some questions never get asked. Good thing, too.

Why do baseball players always scratch themselves?

Is you-know-who on steroids?

Is the ball juiced?

Does what's-his-name wear a rug?

Is golf a sport?

What's a foos?

Why are the Yankees so annoying?

Was Wilt Chamberlain telling the truth?

What do chicks dig more, the long ball or figure skating?

Is the fix really in?

What do they do with the used soap in hotels?

And what about the butter you don't use in a restaurant?

On election days, who are the people working at the polls?

And what do they do when it's not Election Day?

Has anyone actually read *Tuesdays with Morrie*?

Where is Jimmy Hoffa buried?

How come nobody knows?

WORD

▶ Section 3

Where the messy leaves of balderdash are swept into neat piles by the rake of moxie, bagged, and put to the curb.

Why is it called hockey?

Benny Ercolani, chief statistician, NHL: You got me, buddy. **Do you know anyone who might know?** Hmmm. You know, I know a lot of people, but I can't think of anyone. I'm sure there's an answer, though. But it's like, where does football come from? **Well, no, it's not, actually. While I have you, do you want to take a guess?** I don't guess. **What about during guessing games?** Nope. **That's so sad. Better check with Gordie Howe.** *The answering machine of Power Play International:* "Hi. You've reached the company of Colleen and Gordie Howe, Mr. and Mrs. Hockey, hockey's greatest couple. Please leave your message and phone number. The Howes are traveling extensively. Have a great day, God bless, and Howe!" **Yipe!** *Dan Diamond, editor, Total Hockey:* There are several different etymologies. The one you hear most is that it's from the French word *hoquet*, which is a curved stick that gave its name to field hockey. **Sounds plausible.** Another is that in England in the 1400s, the word was used to describe a game played by boys who carried produce in carts called "hocks." The game they played was called hockey. **Why were the carts called "hocks"?**

Because that was a German word for
grape. **Yeah, so?** There were lots of
grapes in the carts. **German grapes?**
In England? Yeah. Uh-huh. Go on.
And in the early 1800s, there was,
in fact, an English colonel stationed
in Nova Scotia, with the last name
Hockey, who had his troops play a
game on ice for exercise. **Hmmm. Did**
Colonel Hockey have a beard? I
don't know.

Shielding the jewels of sagacity from the free kick of foolishness.

Why is it called soccer?

Jim Moorehouse, communications director, U.S. Soccer Federation: Every culture has its own term for the game, like *calcio* in Italy or *labdarugo* in Hungary. **It's all Greek to me.** There it's *podosfairiki.* **Thanks.** Mostly, though, the names for the game essentially translate to foot ball. *O jogo bonito!* Here, the game developed in the early part of the twentieth century, when gridiron football was already pretty well established. **Crush 'em!** Rather than having to explain the difference between the two games, it was easier to simply call it soccer. **Fascinating. So why is it called soccer?** *David Barber, historian, Football Association, England:* "Soccer" derives from "association." **I thought it might.** In the nineteenth century, there were two rival football styles: association football, or soccer, and rugby football. **Gotcha.** One day, around 1870, somebody asked Charles Alcock, the FA secretary, if he was going to play "rugger," a common way for public-school types to refer to rugby. Kids used to add "er" to the end of lots of words. It was a slang thing. **Cheeky.** Alcock said, "Not today, I'm playing soccer." **Cool. So why is it called socc-er?** *Roy Mumme, etymologist, Florida Gulf Coast University:* It's not uncommon for people to reverse

sounds in words to make them easier
to pronounce. It's called metathesis.
Nucular! Association football was
often abbreviated to "assoc. football."
But try saying "assoc." **Ass sock.** Not
very nice. **For some.** By reversing the
syllables, you get "sock ass." **Sure
do.** That's no good either. **For others.**
Changing the "ass" to "er" makes
"soccer," which is more pleasing to
the ear. **But not nearly as much fun!**

Where the cup of uncertainty runneth over with the steadying waters of assuredness.

Why is it called cricket?

Stephen Green, curator, Marylebone Cricket Club Library, London: Nobody knows. **Shocking.** But, of course, there are several theories. **Jolly good.** The most likely explanation is that cricket comes from *crycc*, the Old English word for crook. **What crook?** The shepherds' crook. **What shepherd?** The ones who likely invented the game. **What game?** Cricket. **Crooked shepherds invented cricket?** No, no. "Crook" is the name of the curved stick carried by shepherds. But the Old English word is *crycc*. **'Kay.** In fact, in the earliest English translations of the Bible, the Twenty-third Psalm reads, "The Lord is my shepherd," and so forth, but instead of "Thy rod and thy staff they comfort me," it says "Thy crick comforts me." **Neat. Still leaves me wanting, though.** The shepherds in the Middle Ages had a fair amount of time on their hands, so they invented games. Golf is the prime example. **Way ahead of ya.** [*Ed.'s note: See page 56.*] The theory for cricket is that one shepherd would throw rocks at the wicket gate of another shepherd, which he'd then hit away with his crycc. **The wicket gate?** You Yanks don't have those? **'Fraid not.** Well, I'm not very good at explaining such things. I'll have to refer you to

the dictionary. **Okeydokey.** *Webster's Third New International Dictionary:* "wicket: a small gate or door..." **Door to what?** *Green:* A sheep pen. **Let's see what else that dictionary has to say.** *Webster's:* "cricket (2): [MF *criquet:* goal stakes in old games of bowls, perhaps from *criquer* to crack, of imitative origin; from the sound of the balls striking the stakes.]" **Now wait just a doggone minute ...** *Green:* As I indicated earlier, this is all mere speculation. I mean, none of us were actually there at the time. **Well, as far as we know.**

Where the perplexed deer play with the cocksure antelope, under a cloudless sky.

Why is it called home plate?

Bill Francis, researcher, Baseball Hall of Fame: Nobody knows. **There's a shocker.** The earliest reference is from the Knickerbocker rules, 1845. They refer to "home base," but they don't say why. **Finks!** Early on, home plate was round, which may explain the "plate" part. It was made of marble or iron and painted white. **Like fine china.** At some point, home became a square on point. **Like a diamond.** Right. In a 1900 letter to *The Sporting News*, pitcher Crazy Schmit claimed the five-sided home plate was his idea. **What a nut!** Well, sometime around then they did fill in the corners. **Why?** Maybe it made it easier to call strikes. **And the home part?** Well, there might be a "home" in cricket ... *Selwyn Caesar, second vice president, U. S. of A. Cricket Association:* There isn't. *Francis:* ... or rounders. *Victoria Maddocks, British subject, ESPN The Magazine:* Sorry. No home. **Nuts.** *Red Foley, official scorer, New York Yankees:* Oh, brother. **Tell me about it.** Let's see. Ya got your home plate, your home.run, your home on the range. **True.** Sorry, Guy, can't give ya a solid, meat answer. **No biggie.** I'd tell you to call some other guys, but the guys I know who would know are all dead. **Ah, there's the rub.** *Paul Dickson, author, The*

New Dickson Baseball Dictionary: The concept of "home" is basic to many children's games, hide-and-seek, ring-a-levio, tag. **Not it!** *John Thorn, coeditor, Total Baseball:* Primitive ball games like prisoners base or king ball involved hitting the ball, then venturing into a territory fraught with peril. **Been there.** Like Ulysses on his voyage, you were afforded relief when you reached a "base," which likely derives from "bay," as in harbor. **Nautical!** But the only way to be truly safe is to get back home. **No place like it.** No, sir.

Hoisting the gonfalon of sagacity atop the edifice of pedantry.

Why is it called the World Series?

Red Foley, official scorer, New York Yankees: Just because they play baseball in France, or what have you, doesn't mean they're any good at it. **Darn tootin'!** As for the name itself, I wish I could tell you that Joe Blow came up with it in aught-six. But I can't. **Bummer.** *Sonia, secretary, International Baseball Federation, Switzerland:* I'm sorry, the person you need to ask is on holiday. **Well, you're there.** I'm not the right one for you. **How can we be sure?** Well, perhaps you should come and see us. **Oooh, Sonia ...** *Lance Van Auken, media relations director, Little League Baseball Inc.:* In '47, our first year, we held the National Championship. When we invited foreign teams in '50, we called it the World Series. **Makes sense.** But MLB used it first. *Jeremy Jones, researcher, Baseball Hall of Fame:* In 1884, a challenge game between the Providence Grays and the New York Metropolitans was billed as the Championship of the United States. **Go Grays!** After Providence won ... **Woo-hoo!** ... *Sporting Life* declared them "Champions of the World." **Small world.** It was more of a promotional thing to hype baseball. You know, like saying a tonic is the world's best cure for whooping cough. **Mmmm, Robitussin ...** *John Thorn,*

coeditor, Total Baseball: It's simply the American propensity for unabashed self-aggrandizement. **You can say that again.** Actually, the term "pennant" is even older. **Dish.** With the founding of the National League in 1871, it was decided the team with the most wins would be awarded a whip pennant. **Who's Whip?** That's what pennants do, whip in the breeze to taunt rivals. **Ouch!**

Where the track-worn tires of the witless are changed—fast. With a splash of gas thrown in.

Why is it called a pit stop?

Donald Davidson, historian, Indianapolis Motor Speedway: It comes from France. ***Vraiment?*** Yes, really. In an early Grand Prix race, before World War I, the mechanics dug trenches so they could work under the car. **So the drivers would park the cars over the trenches?** No, they'd park alongside them. **But then the mechanics wouldn't be under the car, would they?** No, I don't suppose they would be. **So why did they dig the trenches?** I don't know. Maybe they were getting ready for the Great War. **Maybe.** *Tony Stewart, Winston Cup driver, No. 20 car:* I have no idea. **But do you have any theories?** Maybe because it's the pits to go in there. **Maybe.** [*Phone rings.*] **Answer Guy here.** *Donald Davidson:* Okay, here's the deal. **Dish it, Don.** The 1908 French Grand Prix was in Dieppe, a very long course, about 40 miles a lap. There was a refueling depot, but it was right in front of the grandstand. They were worried the fans wouldn't be able to see. So they dug a pit for crews to stand in while they waited. When the cars came in, they'd climb out. **So the first pit stop was literally a pit. When did the term become popular over here?** Well, I know we were using it at Indy by 1911. **Gee, word traveled**

fast back then. Hey, wait—the
French wouldn't have called it a
"pit stop." They'd have called it a
fosse d'arret. Or something like
that. How do they say "pit stop"
in France? *Receptionist, Automobile
Club de Monaco, Monaco:* Peet layne.
Really? *Oui.* **That's ridiculous. I'm
heading back to the trenches.**
*Jeffrey Cheatham, Winston Cup pit
board man, No. 77 car:* Before they
had hydraulic lifts, mechanics dug
pits in the shop floor. The term just
carried over to the races. **Was it the
pits to go in there?** Maybe.

Where the good guy of perception mixes it up with the bad guy of opacity—and kicks some butt!

Why is a strikeout called a K?

John Thorn, coeditor, Total Baseball: Henry Chadwick invented the score-keeping system in the 1860s. He used S for single, D for double, like that. One of the few surviving symbols is the K. **And ...?** They wouldn't say "strikeout," they'd say the batter had "struck three times and was out." **That's a mouthful.** S was taken, so Chadwick chose K, the last letter in "struck." **What about the backward K for a called third strike?** *Red Foley, official scorer, New York Yankees:* Jeez. I've been working on this one for years. **Any luck?** Nope. All that matters is that the scorer knows what each symbol means. I had a friend who put NT next to a hit if the fielder made a good effort. **NT?** Nice try. *Frank Vito, researcher, Baseball Hall of Fame:* This is a lame question. **Excuse me?** C'mon, it's a K because of the way the word sounds. Strike. I knew that before I started working here. **Oh, yeah? Well, what about Henry Chadwick?** What about him? **He invented it.** So? **So it has nothing to do with the way the word sounds.** Chadwick chose K because it's the most prominent sound in "strike." **Not according to my sources.** Your sources? This is the Hall of Fame, pal. **What's your problem?** I don't have a problem.

What's your problem? **I just want the answer.** What are you, Answer Guy? **As a matter of fact, yes.** That's what they call me on my softball team: Frank "Answer Guy" Vito. **A nickname does not Answer Guy make.** Do you know why they call lefties "southpaws"? **Don't change the subject.** Home plate was always on the western side of the field ... **Don't care ...** to keep the sun out of the hitters' eyes ... **Sure, sure ...** A lefty threw from the south side of home. Not bad, huh? **Whatever. But do you know what NT means?** No clue. **Ha!**

Where the toro of investigation charges the matador of complacency— and gores him mortally.

Why is the center of a target called a bull's-eye?

Catherine McCullough, director of programs, United States Archery: We call it the inner ten. **Why?** Well, it's the innermost ring on the target, and it's worth ten points. **Fascinating.** Actually, in the book *Archery*, Robert Elmer defines bull's-eye as, "the golden center of a target, or the golden part of the bull's-eye." Whether or not bulls' eyes are golden I can't say. *Coleman Cooney, director, California Academy of Tauromaquia:* That's Spanish for bull fighting. **Thanks.** The answer, however, is no. **Nerts.** *Kristen Wolfred, communications coordinator, National Dart Association:* The earliest targets were upturned tree trunks. That's where the rings come from. **Aha!** When the game moved indoors, beer barrel bottoms became ideal targets. **Bottoms up!** There was a cork in the center of the barrel bottom, which is why bull's-eye is synonymous with cork. **But why is cork synonymous with bull's-eye?** No clue. *Steve Perrault, director of defining, Merriam-Webster, Inc.:* "Center of a target" dates to 1833. But the oldest meaning is nautical, from 1753, and refers to "A little dark cloud, reddish in the middle, chiefly appearing about the Cape of Good Hope." **Shiver me**

timbers! From 1789, we have "Bull's-eye: a small pulley in the form of a ring, having a rope round the outer edge and a hole in the middle for another rope to slide in." **Yar.** By 1825, a round piece of glass inserted in a ship's deck to illuminate lower decks is known as a bull's-eye. **Me hearties.** Another common meaning refers to a bulge in a sheet of blown glass. **Aye!** So you have these disparate meanings, all vaguely referring to a circular shape in the center of something. Calling that an "eye" is an ancient coinage, but why it would be a bull's eye, I can't say. **Argh.** It's also the name of an Australian fish. **Well, then, that explains it.** *Cooney:* Bulls have always been significant symbolically. The pharaohs called themselves the Bulls, and bulls are sacred to Hindus. **True.** In Western cultures, bulls were revered for their strength and ferocity and as a symbol of sexual potency. **Yipe!** As we've become more industrialized, much of that symbolism has been lost. **Consider it found.**

Filling the doughnut holes of doubt with the dough of certainty, thereby creating a Danish.

Why do golfers yell "fore"?

Receptionist, PGA Tour media office: It's a warning to other golfers when someone hits an errant shot. **No kidding. But why "fore," why not, say, "two"?** We don't have that information. **Nobody knows?** I'm sure *somebody* knows, we just don't have that information. In words. **Do you have it some other way?** In the dictionary. Would you like me to fax it to you? **No thanks, I think I can rustle up a dictionary.** *Karen Bednarski, director, World Golf Hall of Fame:* It's Scottish, short for "before." **Before what?** Before you get conked on the head, I guess. **Good one.** Thanks. The first citing, according to *The Historical Dictionary of Golfing Terms*, is from 1819, in *Blackwood's Edinburgh Magazine:* " … and clearing, with an imperious 'fore,' the way." **Nice syntax.** *Jason Zuback, four-time World Long Driving Champion:* It's really a courtesy, when a wayward shot has potential to put someone in jeopardy. **Do your shots put people in jeopardy?** No, I hit it pretty straight. **Yeah, yeah. Drive for show …** There are different kinds of "fores," you know. **Do tell.** There's the casual "fore," to get somebody's attention. Then there's the more emphatic "fore!" which indicates extreme urgency. **Gotcha.** *Barry Kerr,*

managing director, *Heritage Golf of St. Andrews, Scotland:* Over here, "the fore" is anything in front of you. It's a quicker way of saying, "Mind yer hede, ya daft doommy." **Aye.** *Andy Mutch, curator, USGA Museum and Library Golf House:* It's from Old English, "beware before." Remember how the British Army used to stand in lines when they marched into battle? **If only I could forget.** Guys in the back row would yell "fore" when they fired their weapons so the guys in the front would know to duck. **The daft doommies.**

Where the piled leaves of obfuscation are scattered by the jumping ruffian of elucidation.

Why do quarterbacks say "hike"?

Alan Grant, ex-NFLer, ESPN The Magazine: Hike: To move, pull, or raise with a sudden motion. **Wow!** It's called a dictionary, Guy. Look into it. **Alan, Alan, what have I done to make you treat me so disrespectfully?** Anyway, nobody says "hike." It's "hut." **Why?** For the Answer Guy you ask a lot of questions. **What about "bluuue forty-twooo"?** That's an audible. Get with it. **Must you hurt me so?** *Saleem Choudhry, researcher, Pro Football Hall of Fame:* I think I know this one! **Get out!** No really, I read an article once. I'll find it and call you back. **Go for it.** *Kent Stephens, curator, College Football Hall of Fame:* Walter Camp invented the snap. **But did he say "hike"?** Can't say. But he did come up with signal calling. **Hut-one, hut-two?** Something like that. Camp's the father of American football, largely because of the scrimmage rule. **Scrimmage rule?** It established that one team has possession of the ball. It's a military term for a small battle or skirmish. **Wait a minute: ten-hut! Maybe "hut" is an army word.** *Louise Friend, Military History Institute:* In my 25-plus years—and how many more than 25 is none of your

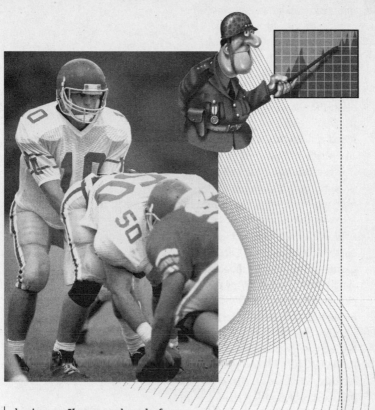

business—I've never heard of a connection between military and football cadences. **Okay, then.** *Choudhry:* Sorry, no dice. **What happened?** The story's a fabrication. **Lay it on me anyway.** Okay, but don't quote me. **Done.** Back in the day, this school had three sheds behind the end zone. When the QB wanted his receiver to run a particular route, he'd tell him which shed to run toward: hut one, hut two, or hut three. *Grant:* Now, that's cool. **Take a hike, Al.**

Checking the sprites of mischief into the boards of discipline.

Who came up with "puck"?

Joy Kalfus, publicist, NHL: There's no good answer for that. **Yet.** Try calling In Glas. They make pucks for us. *Cindy, receptionist, In Glas, Inc.:* Pucks come from Slovakia. **And?** And that's all I can tell you. **Why?** Because that's all I know. **Fair enough.** *Earl Zuckerman, sports information director, McGill University, Montreal:* The French word is *les rondelles*, which means rings, as in *les rondelles d'oignons*. **That's good eatin'.** Of course, most Quebecois simply say "*le puck.*" **Mais oui.** They also use the word "puck" in hurling. **I believe that's "puke," Earl.** No, no, hurling. It's a sport in Ireland. **You're telling me.** *Brendan Walsh, Answer Guy's Irish friend:* Hurling is like lacrosse, only savage. **Grrrr.** But the ball's not a puck, it's a *sliotar*. **Och!** There is something called a "puck out," though. **And what's that?** It's when the goalie has the ball and he pucks it out. **Glad we cleared that up.** *Dan Diamond, editor, Total Hockey:* Some people like to think it derives from the devilish fairy, Puck, in Shakespeare's *A Midsummer Night's Dream*. You know, because the puck can be tricky to deal with. **Lord, what fools these mortals be.** Quite. Ice hockey was first played outside British garrisons in what is now Nova Scotia and Ontario. **With ya.** Many

soldiers were of Irish decent. In fact, the game was sometimes called "hurling on ice." *Yeesh.* Soldiers would play with whatever they found, an old boot heel, a piece of wood, even frozen dung. **What a game.** In Gaelic, "puck" means to strike or hit, as in "Do ya want a puck in the puss?" **Yipe!** They may simply have transferred the action onto the object. **Puck the puck!** Exactly.

Squeezing the tart lemons of stupidity into the sweet lemonade of lucidity.

What's the deal with the hat trick?

Dan Diamond, editor, Total Hockey: It's rooted in cricket. **No, really...** A lot of Canadian games came out of English sporting clubs. There's probably a connection to the British tradition of being "capped." You'd be given an embroidered hat when you were selected for the national team. **Embroidered hats? We're talkin' hockey here.** *Jane Rodney, resource center coordinator, NHL Hall of Fame:* There are two theories, really, but we stand by the cricket version. **Enough with the cricket. Could I please have the real answer?** Well, there's the story of Sammy Taft, the Toronto hatmaker who gave a free hat to any player who scored at least three goals at Maple Leaf Gardens. **Now we're talkin'.** By that account, it started in the '40s when Taft gave Alex Kaleta of the Blackhawks a new fedora. But we know it was in cricket long before. **Yeah, right. Nice try.** *Barbara Davidson, PR assistant, Chicago Blackhawks:* The Kaleta story is as good as any. There's also reference to fans "passing the hat" when a player scored three goals. **Beautiful.** Of course it all derives from crick ... *Benny Ercolani, chief statistician, NHL:* There's no definite answer, but there is a hat trick in cricket. **Et tu, Benny?** If you get three consecutive

wickets, and knock the thing off there, you get a hat. **Fine. It comes from cricket. But why a hat?** *Stephen Green, curator, Marylebone Cricket Club Library, London:* Oh, that's very easy. **Don't push me, Stephen.** If a bowler took three wickets on three consecutive balls, he'd be given a top hat. **But why?!** Well, it is nice to get a new hat. **Yeah, I guess it is.**

Warning the Caesar of fact about the senators of fiction.

Why do they say "top of the key" in hoops?

Kaan Guven, NBA media relations assistant: That's where the guy is. **What guy?** Whatever guy they're talking about. **Who?** Whoever says "top of the key." **Right. And why do they say that?** Because that's where he is, at the top of the key. **What key?** You know, the key, the lane, the paint. **Uh-huh. And why is it called the key?** I don't know. *Doug Stark, librarian and archivist, Basketball Hall of Fame:* The lane used to be narrower. With the foul circle on top, it looked like a key. **Why was the lane narrow?** I don't know. **Can you find out?** I guess, but I'd have to do research. **Isn't that your job?** Yeah.. **Thought so.** *Bill Walton, Hall of Fame hoopster:* We should say "key hole," because that's what it used to look like. Of course, now that they've widened the lane, it looks more like a water tower. **True, true.** *Marty Blake, NBA director of scouting:* It's like "cagers." **It is?** In the old days, traveling teams would encounter what you might call rabid fans. **Yipe!** The courts were surrounded with chicken wire, like a cage. The players were called cagers. **And somebody had a key to this cage?** Could be. **I'm so confused.** *Bill Himmelman, NBA historian:* The key was introduced in response to the pivot ... **Oh, jeez ...**

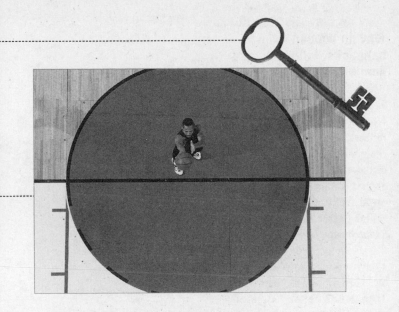

Hall of Famer Dutch Dehnert would stand below the foul line and have guys cut off him. It was indefensible. **Clearly.** So they added the three-second rule and put in the lane. **Clever.** Then they widened it for George Mikan, later for Wilt. **Why?** To push the big guys back from the hoop. **Beauty.** By the way, I read that bowling thing. [*Ed.'s note: See page 46.*] **And?** You mentioned the German word *kegel*, but didn't say that that's why bowlers are called "keglers." **I didn't know bowlers were called keglers.** Oh, sure, like "cagers" in hoops. **Say no more.**

Where answers to the most vexing questions are uncovered like a ball off the bat of Barry Bonds.

Why do we call them halfbacks, fullbacks, and quarterbacks?

Saleem Choudhry, researcher, Pro Football Hall of Fame: Simple. The fullback is the full distance back from the line, the halfback is half that distance, the quarterback is a quarter of that distance. **But fullbacks line up in front of halfbacks, Saleem ... Hello? Better call the Saints.** *Dean Kleinschmidt, longtime New Orleans trainer:* Golly, I don't know. But I got a guy workin' here who's 75 years old, been around the game 54 years. Sarge. **Who?** Warren "Sarge" Arial. **Oh.** *Sarge:* It's a breakdown of fractions. **Get out.** Yup. In the old days, the fullback was the last guy back there. See, Pop Warner invented the single wing and the double wing and on those, the fullback was the middle man ... **But ...** then in 1939, the Bears used the T, where the two halfbacks were back there with the fullback ... **Sarge ...** and back in '26, General Neyland, head coach at Tennessee, invented the sideline kickoff return, and the thing you oughta remember is ... **Sarge! ...** deep-crotch pants, which had zippers, came later, but we don't use 'em anymore 'cause they get rusty. **Gotta go.** Hope I didn't mess you up. *Spike Dykes, head coach, Texas Tech:* Don't

have a clue. I think they call the fullback that 'cause he's so damn big. Try the College Football Hall of Fame. **Okay.** *Kent Stephens, collections manager, College Football Hall of Fame:* It comes from Welsh rugby, which, in the 1800s, called guys behind the front line "backs"— fullbacks, halfbacks, quarterbacks, even three-quarters backs—according to where they lined up. American football derives from rugby, and some of the position names stuck, even if they didn't make sense anymore. **What about "special teams"? They're no more special than the rest of the team, doesn't seem fair.** Probably started in the '60s. **Yeah, the '60s were weird.** Yeah.

Sweeping the floor of "hmmm?" with the broom of "you don't say."

What's so "special" about special teams?

Alan Grant, ex-NFLer, current Answer Guy colleague: They're certainly "different" teams, but I don't know about special. **"Different" how?** You're "Answer Guy," you figure it out. **Not "helpful," Al.** *Kent Stephens, collections manager, College Football Hall of Fame:* I'll take a wild guess and say it's a pro thing, not a college thing. **You go, Kent.** Until the mid-'60s, college had very restrictive substitution rules. **Such as?** If you came out in the first quarter, you couldn't come back in until the second quarter. Everybody had to do everything. It was one-platoon football. **Sixty-minute men?** Right. *Saleem Choudhry, researcher, Pro Football Hall of Fame:* Oh, jeez. **What's wrong?** Another season of silly questions from Answer Guy. **One man's "silly" is another man's "profound."** Yeah, right. Anyway, "special teams" just means not offense and not defense. **Sounds like "neutral teams" to me.** Bet you didn't know that Dick Vermeil was the first special teams coach, with the Rams in '69. *Rick Smith, PR director, Rams:* Head coach George Allen hired Dick. Until then, special teams were handled by an assistant. **Did they call them special teams?** Don't know. I do know kickoff teams were called

suicide squads. **Yipe!** *Dick Vermeil, retired NFL coach:* They were called coverage teams, and there were schemes and players called flying wedges and wedge busters. But you'd have to credit Allen with calling them "special." **But what's so "special" about them?** *Steve Tasker, retired special teams specialist:* Well, it's a totally different game. **How so?** First, you're purposely giving the ball to your opponent. **Hey, yeah!** Second, guys are running 60 yards downfield and slamming into each other. **Yes, that is "special."**

Where "How should I know?" meets "What are you asking me for?" and agrees to disagree.

Shouldn't the Toronto Maple Leafs be the Toronto Maple Leaves?

Michael Miranda, reader of ESPN The Magazine, Kauai, Hawaii: Hey, that's my question! **Says you.** But I e-mailed you. **Whatever. Who else did you ask?** My high school teachers. They said it was some kind of Canadian thing. **We'll see about that.** *Maria, research librarian, National Library of Canada:* It's not a Canadian thing, per se, but the Maple Leaf is an important national symbol. **And why's that?** It goes back a long way, likely to aboriginal people who harvested maple sap every spring. **So they could have been the Toronto Maple Saps?** I really can't say. **Sure you can!** Is this some kind of joke? **Yes, Maria. Yes it is.** Well, all right then. *Dave Griffiths, media relations coordinator, Toronto Maple Leafs:* Conn Smythe changed the name from the St. Patricks to the Maple Leafs when he bought the team in '27. **And why's that?** He had a lot of patriotic pride. **Yes, but why Leafs?** He was in World War I. Canadian soldiers wore Maple Leaf armbands. I suppose he thought calling them the Leaves would diminish the symbolism. *James HiDuke, "Dr. Grammar," University of Northern Iowa:* Webster's recognizes "leafs" as an acceptable pluralization.

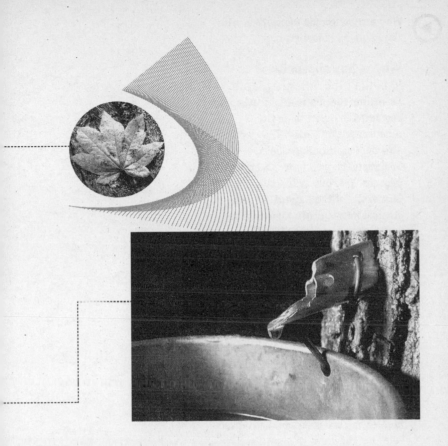

American Heritage does not. **Mercy!** When dealing with titles, it's often best to leave it alone—the hell with grammar! **You're a credit to the profession, Doc.** *Dan Diamond, editor, Total Hockey:* "Leafs" with an "f" predates Smythe. There was a local hockey team—even a baseball team—called the Maple Leafs. **Some kind of Canadian thing, eh?** Nah. It probably just looked better on the sweater.

Filling the curricula of curiosity with the syllabi of gumption.

Why is Sox misspelled?

Peter Chase, media relations, Boston Red Sox: They used to be the Americans. **That's nice.** They were also the Puritans, Speedboys, Somersets, Plymouth Rocks, and Pilgrims. **Yes, but ...** In 1907, the Beaneaters of the National League stopped wearing their signature red socks because manager Fred Tenney believed the dye caused blood poisoning. **Way ahead of ya.** [*Ed.'s note: See page 58.*] Red Sox owner John Taylor said, "From now on we'll wear red stockings, and I'm grabbing that name Red Sox!" **So he was a lousy speller?** No clue. *Eric Phillips, baseball information coordinator, Chicago White Sox:* The Cubs were originally the White Stockings. **Oh, jeez.** But later became the Colts. **Why me?** When their manager, Cap Anson, who was known as Pop, got fired, they were called the Orphans. **Fine. Now about the Sox?** Comiskey brought the American League team here in 1901 and revived the name White Stockings. **Sox, Eric, why Sox?** In 1902 they became the White Sox. **Is it me?** *Matt Silverman, associate publisher, Total Baseball:* The Indians were originally the Blues. **Not helpful.** And later the Naps, after Nap Lajoie became their star. **Are you *trying* to annoy me?** A 1915 newspaper contest resulted in the

name Indians, supposedly inspired by an old Cleveland Spiders player, Louis Sockalexis, a Native American. **Sock! You said sock!** He had a bad drinking problem, and played only 94 games in his career. **Will someone please shoot me?** For headlines, the *Chicago Tribune* shortened "Stockings" to "Sox." **Aha!** *Colleen Vander Hye, researcher, Chicago Tribune:* To help immigrants, newspapers often spelled words phonetically, like "clue" was "clew"; "through," "thru." **Sweet.** Columnists Carl Green and I. E. Sanborn are credited with "Sox." **Pyoor jeenyus.**

Where the stallions of conjecture run free in the fields of speculation.

What's the story on charley horse?

Al Green, PR chairman, National Athletic Trainers' Association: A charley horse is a contusion or bruise resulting in intramuscular bleeding. It generally relates to the thigh. **What's it have to do with horses?** Not much, I guess. You know, a lot of this stuff is regional. Like when I was athletic trainer at the University of Kentucky, kids would come in and say they "creeled" their ankle. It took me a week to realize that "creel" meant "sprain." **Interesting.** Then they'd ask for a brown bag and vinegar to get the swelling down, but that's a different story. **I'm sure it is. Now, about charley horse.** *Paul Dickson, author, The New Dickson Baseball Dictionary:* There are so many stories, it's impossible to know where it comes from. **How about a guess?** One popular theory is that it comes from the name Charley Esper, a left-handed pitcher who walked like a lame horse. **Sounds good.** But the expression was already in widespread use in 1894 when Esper joined the Orioles. **Drat.** Other sources credit Cub infielder Joe Quest, the son of a blacksmith, who compared limping players to his father's old white horse, named Charlie. **Hmmm.** Another story, also from Baltimore, says that several players bet on a horse named Charley

who was leading the whole race, then pulled up lame in the final stretch. **Blast it!** The following day, a baserunner pulled a tendon in his leg and was likened by one of the coaches to "our old Charley horse." **Now *that* I like.** You know, the search for the source of the term is nearly as old as the term itself. **I didn't know.** Lexicographer Barry Popik found a story in the June 15, 1887 edition of the *St. Louis Post-Dispatch* that says, "the name is said to owe its origin to the fact that a player afflicted with it, when attempting to run, does so much after the fashion of a boy astride a wooden horse, sometimes called a charley horse." **Whoa is me.**

Speed of lightning, roar of thunder,
fighting all who rob or plunder—
Answer Guy! Answer Guy!

Why are they called underdogs?

Kevin, Hard Rock Hotel & Casino sports book, Las Vegas: A horse named Underdog beat Man o' War in the '20s. *Tony Sinisi, Las Vegas Sports Consultants:* That horse was upset. **Well sure, but ...** No, the horse was named Upset. He beat Man o' War in 1919. **Was Upset an underdog?** Big time. It's the only race Man o' War ever lost. *Howard Schwartz, Gamblers Book Club, Las Vegas:* Man o' War's jockey was drunk. **Bummer.** Anyway, here's what *The Dictionary of Gambling & Gaming* says: "Underdog: In a gambling game or sporting contest, an entry thought to have little chance to win. See also 'dark horse.'" **Okay.** "A horse not favored to win." **Duh!** Here's the citation, 1829. From a book called *Turf Expositor:* "Forth's two horses were nothing thought of, particularly Frederick, the winner. He was a dark horse who shed an unpleasant and irksome light upon the visual orbs of the knowing ones by winning the great stake." **I see ... I think.** Say, how about a story on gambling? You know how much money is gambled on sports? **Well, I ...** Wouldn't you like to know if an NFL game was fixed? **Yes, but ...** The FBI shops with us, pal! **I'm sure they do.** *Steve Perrault, director of defining, Merriam-Webster, Inc.:* Underdog dates

to 1887. Defined as "the beaten dog in a dog fight." The shift in meaning from "already defeated" to "expected to lose" first appears in 1961. **Sound right, Joe?** *Joe Harris, creator of Underdog character:* All I know is that in '63 there was a fall from innocence after Kennedy. People wanted to laugh at heroes. Underdog's a hero, but he's clumsy and forgetful. You knew he'd trip and fall or do something dumb ... **Like Man o' War's jockey?** ... so you just had to root for him. **Everybody loves an underdog.** Indeed.

Answering the da-nana-nun-da-na of inquiry with the "Charge!" of scholarship.

Why are we called fans?

Paul Dickson, author, The New Dickson Baseball Dictionary: At early English prizefights, around the 1820s, there was a crowd of decadent gentlemen who drank, cavorted with prostitutes, and wore ruffled shirts and lots of perfume. **My kind of guys!** Pierce Egan, the first real sportswriter, called them the "Fancy Boys." I believe "fan" is a corruption of "fancy." **Fancy that.** But I don't have the smoking gun. **Huh?** There's no published evidence that "fancy" was ever shortened to "fan." **So?** So I have to go with "fan" as a clipping of "fanatic." **Why?** Because there's hard evidence to back it up. **Hit me.** The story comes from sportswriter Ted Sullivan. He claimed that in 1883, Charles Comiskey called an enthusiast who visited the Cardinals clubhouse a "fanatic," which Sullivan shortened to "fan." The term was in widespread use soon after. *John Thorn, coeditor, Total Baseball:* Prior to "fan," enthusiasts were most often called "bugs" or "kranks." Both terms connote a sickness that infected people with a love of the game. **Baseball fever?** Exactly. But, you know, spectators often fanned themselves to keep cool. Some scorecards even came affixed with wooden handles. **The wave!** It's plausible that the implement wielded

by spectators gave its name to the spectators themselves. *Steve Perrault, director of defining, Merriam-Webster, Inc.:* We say it's *probably* short for "fanatic", but we can't know for sure. **You're killing me, Stevie.** The earliest citing is from 1682, in a poem called "New News from Bedlam." **Crazy.** "To be here Nurs'd up, Loyal Fanns to defame, And damn all Dissenters on purpose for gain." **Fanns?** They could spell things however they wanted back then. **Phascinating.**

Where the cows of ignorance jump over the moon of bliss.

Why are pitchers kept in a bullpen?

Paul Dickson, author, The New Dickson Baseball Dictionary: This is a very contentious issue. **Bring it on!** The first citing of "bullpen" as the place where pitchers warm up was in the December 1915 issue of *Baseball Magazine*. **But why "bullpen"?** Well, relief pitching emerged around the turn of the century. At that time, nearly every ballpark in the country featured a Bull Durham tobacco sign—a giant bull-shaped billboard— affixed to the outfield wall. **Smokin'.** All the games were played during the day, and relievers warmed up in the shadow of the bull. Over time, that area became known as the bullpen. *John Thorn, coeditor, Total Baseball:* That's horsesh ... **oes!** Relief pitching was virtually unknown until the 1890s, and "bullpen" was in use as early as 1870. It referred to the roped-off area in foul territory from where late arriving fans could watch the game. **Moooo!** As relief pitching developed, the term bullpen transferred meaning from a place for fans to stand to a place for pitchers to warm up. **Any idea why?** Well, fan bullpens were up the lines, which is likely where the pitchers were, too. Like in Wrigley. *Steve Perrault, director of defining, Merriam-Webster, Inc.:* "Bullpen" is almost always used

metaphorically, not as reference to a pen for <u>male cows</u>. **Curious.** In early usage, around 1850, it referred to a variety of enclosures, most commonly ones in which prisoners were confined. **Why bull, and not, say, pig?** It makes sense for prisoners, in that they're dangerous and need to be confined, like a bull, for safety's sake. But there's no evidence that relief pitchers are dangerous. **Ever been to Shea?**

Where truth, like good veal, is pounded until tender.

Why is one under par called a birdie?

Barry Kerr, managing director, Heritage Golf of St. Andrews, Scotland: I'll pass on that one, lad. The story cannot be told over the phone. **Why's that?** Let's say it's of a rather rude nature. **Give us a hint.** Well, do you know the gesture "flipping the bird"? **Heard of it.** It comes from the Battle of Agincourt. [*Ed.'s note: England vs. France, 1415.*] Our archers pulled back their bow strings with their middle fingers. **So "birdie" comes from flipping the bird?** I didn't say that! It just might shed a wee bit of light. **Not really, but thanks.** *Evan Rothman, editor, Golf Retailer magazine:* Funny you should ask. **Why?** Because I know the answer. **Is it of a rude nature?** No. **Why? Skip it.** Around the turn of the century, Abner Smith, at the Atlantic City Country Club, hit a 2-iron that bounced, like, two inches from the cup. A buddy said, "Man, what a bird that was." When he sunk the putt, they called it a birdie. I don't know what the hell "bird" means, though. *Kris Pujda, administrative assistant, Atlantic City Country Club:* Back then, "bird" described something good. But let me look in the book. **There's a book?** Yeah, *Birth of the Birdie*. We put it out for our centennial in '97. **Happy birthday.** Thanks. [*reading*] In

December 1903, Smith blah, blah, blah ... and one of his group was moved to say, "That was a bird of a shot." **Yeah, yeah, but how did everybody else find out?** Visitors learned the local term and spread it around the world. **Who knew A. C. was such a golf hub. Got a line on "eagle"?** I guess it's just a really majestic birdie. **Indeed. What about "bogey"?** *Karen Bednarski, director, World Golf Hall of Fame:* It's complicated. In the 1880s, they standardized scoring. An English guy, Major Charles Wellman, described par as "a regular Bogey Man." A real pain. Soon, bogey meant missing par. It's from a song, "Hush, hush, hush, here comes the Bogey Man." **Hmmm. Catchy.**

Where the gutters of triflery are converted to the channels of significance.

Why do they say "strike" and "spare" in bowling?

Mark Miller, public relations, American Bowling Congress: Some people contend that the one-line symbol for a spare should be used for a strike, and the two-line symbol for a strike should be used for a spare because that's how many balls you have to throw for each. **Makes sense. But why "strikes" and "spares"?** Nobody knows. **Sad, really.** *Al Loreto, former pin setter and Answer Guy's father-in-law:* Aren't you the Answer Man? **Answer *Guy*, Al.** So why don't you have the answer? **I'm looking for it.** So you're Looking-for-the-Answer Guy? **Not helpful.** I used to be a pin setter. **Yeah, I know.** Ten cents a game. **Ka-ching!** I could work two lanes at once. But then the automatic pin setters came along and that was that. **Tough break. Now about strikes and spares?** How should I know? And by the way, most people don't know how to keep score, anyway. **No wonder.** *Travis Boley, curator, International Bowling Museum and Hall of Fame:* Thomas Curtis came up with the 300-point scoring system around 1895. **So I'm told.** [*Ed.'s note: See page 22.*] As for "strike" and "spare," nobody knows. **Nobody?** I've asked the people who should know, and they don't. **Well,**

shouldn't *you* know? I suppose.
Bowling does have a very interesting
history, though. **I'm sure it does.**
The first reference to bowling in the
New World is from a law passed in
Jamestown in 1608. **What's it say?**
No bowling. *Jake Schmidt, historian,*
Bowlers Journal International:
Bowling has German roots, and we
think that strike comes from the
German, *streik,* which means a blow
or a hit. As for spare, nobody knows.
Way ahead of ya. The best we can
figure, it refers to the spare pins left
over after the first ball. **The ones**
that were spared? I suppose.
Incidentally, the expression "Drive
for show, putt for dough" really
comes from bowling. Except it's
"Strike for show, spare for dough."
Golf stole it. **Turkeys!**

Suplexing the bad guy of mystery into the turnbuckle of discovery.

Who's Nelson?

Mike Fazioli, managing editor, WWF Raw magazine: Excuse me? **You know, full nelson, half nelson, like that.** Oh, *that* Nelson. No idea. *John Porco, PR coordinator, WWF:* Nobody knows. **Come on, nobody?** Not even Classy Freddie Blassie. **Wow.** *Alan Sharp, PR director, WCW:* We invented it. **Really?** No. But it's all I've got. **Fair enough.** It's illegal in college, but we allow it. **Shocking.** There's no eye gouging, hair pulling, or throwing a guy over the top rope, though. **Pity.** *David Ruth, spokesperson for Jesse Ventura, governor of Minnesota:* I asked the governor and he responded simply, "Mr. Nelson." **Can I talk to him?** No. *Gary Abbott, communications director, USA Wrestling:* It's Lord Nelson. He was one of those guys who went out and discovered, you know, in boats. **You mean British Admiral Lord Horatio Nelson?** Yeah, him. *Shirley Ito, librarian, Amateur Athletic Foundation of Los Angeles:* Apparently, after Nelson's victories in the Napoleonic Wars [*Ed.'s note: 1790s–early 1800s.*], the English used the phrase "put the nelson on him" to mean dominate an opponent. **Nelson wrestled?** *Matthew Sheldon, curator of manuscripts, Royal Naval Museum, Portsmouth, England:* No. He was really rather sickly. And he lost an arm in '97, so he couldn't have

done a full nelson if he wanted to. *Yvonne Ball, administrator, British Amateur Wrestling Association:* I don't think it has anything to do with Lord Nelson. **Oh no?** I think it comes from the town Nelson. In Lancashire. Lancashire-style wrestling, or catch-as-catch-can, has had a profound effect on wrestling. **Indeed.** *Brian, attendant, Marsden Park Pro Shop, Nelson:* Um, this is a golf course. **I know, but it's the only number I could find.** So what do you want to know? **Who's Nelson?** That's the silliest question I've ever heard. **Okay then, who's Mulligan?** Now that's a good question.

Where the shanks of delusion are granted a reprieve at redemption's tee.

Who's Mulligan?

Derek, refreshment coordinator, Mulligan's Pub, New York City: Why do you want to know? **It's what I do.** Fair enough. It's a personal name. **What person?** I don't know. **Oh.** There is a term in golf, though. Is that what you're after? **'Tis.** Can't help you there. I'm Irish, and it's a mortal sin to take a mulligan in Ireland. **That reminds me …** [*Ed.'s note: Cue harp, fuzzy lens.*] *Frank, Answer Guy's brother, first tee, Waterville, Ireland:* Damn! … I'm hitting another. *Patrick, Frank's caddy:* As you like. *Frank:* Back home, this is called a mulligan. What's it called here? *Patrick:* Cheating. [*Ed.: End flashback.*] **Whoa! That was weird.** *Barry Kerr, managing director, Heritage Golf of St. Andrews, Scotland:* We Scots take a more starched-collar approach to the rules. **Indeed.** Golf was first played before Masonic meetings. **You mean the ancient society of Freemasons that secretly rules the world?** I didn't say that! Let's just say they're businessmen with the means to lubricate the wheels of industry. **Yes. Let's.** *Rand Jerris, librarian and historian, USGA Golf House Museum:* David B. Mulligan is the most widely accepted progenitor of the term. He had a regular foursome at the Country Club de Montréal in the '20s, but he was

the only one with a car. ***Oo-kay.*** He drove his buddies to the course. On the way, they had to cross a rickety old bridge. **Spooky.** By the time they got to the first tee, Mulligan was still shaking from the ride. If he hit a bad shot, his buddies let him hit another. **Sporting.** He joined Winged Foot in the '30s and brought the practice with him. *Jay Nieporte, pro shop manager, Winged Foot G.C., Mamaroneck, N.Y.:* Mulligan became a member in '37. There was no practice range. If his first drive was bad, he'd hit another. **Sinner.** He called it a "correction shot." Everyone else called it a "mulligan." **Well, everyone except the Irish.**

Answer Guy Stone Said to Be Fraud

MONTICELLO, N.Y— The archaeology world was rocked today by charges that the so-called Answer Guy Stone, hailed as one of the most important antiquity finds in decades, is nothing more than a hoax. "The so-called Answer Guy Stone, one of the most important antiquity finds in decades, is a hoax and nothing more," writes Ezekiel scholars to "come out to the parking lot—you won't believe what I found." Ironically, they did believe him, although what the scholars saw in the back of Tuttle's beat-up Toyota pickup was almost too good to be true: a 6,000-square-centimeter slab of black basalt whose stylized carvings gave strong indications that the stone was the first

"THE SO-CALLED ANSWER GUY STONE, ONE OF THE MOST IMPORTANT ANTIQUITY FINDS IN DECADES, IS A HOAX AND NOTHING MORE"

Breakey in the most recent issue of *Archaeology Yesterday*.

The scholarly journal also reports that Dr. Jonathan Tuttle, discoverer of the Answer Guy Stone, was unavailable for comment. When contacted for this story, Tuttle responded similarly. "I can't talk now," he said.

Tuttle, 78, burst onto the international stage last year when, at a conference in Alexandria, Egypt, he appeared at a cocktail party and cajoled several visiting known Answer Guy column. Answer Guy, of course, is the idiosyncratic detective whose sleuthing for *ESPN The Magazine* has revolutionized the world of sports inquiry. The reclusive gumshoe's origins have long been a mystery, but Tuttle's find suggested that Answer Guy has been probing the mysteries of sport for much longer than had previously been assumed. The Answer Guy Stone was carbon-dated to approximately 3100 B.C., making

Found and lost: Tuttle's "discovery" is the latest in a career rocked by scandal.

Chariot races like these were not a staple of Sumerian culture.

the rock carving more than 5,100 years old, a good 5,095 years older than the next oldest Answer Guy reference.

To be sure, skeptics had their doubts from the beginning. But the question on the Stone, *Why do Sumerian chariot drivers wear pleated skirts?*, the creative use of sources (Answer Guy's brother-in-law, a chariot mechanic), and some familiar phraseology ("Nobody knows") suggested the oblong slab was authentic.

Tuttle—who claimed to have dragged the half-ton object from a dig near Allepo, Syria—was feted from continent to continent, and Madagascar. Only last month, he was named to the prestigious Waggoner History Chair at the Egan Academy in suburban Dallas. All would have remained as it was had not a reporter from *Archaeology Yesterday* tried to verify the Stone's authenticity as part of a commemorative "Total Tuttle" issue slated for publication later this year. Almost immediately, however, problems arose, not least the fact that there were no chariot races—or chariots— in third millennium B.C. Sumeria. "More importantly," explained Breakey, "I called Answer Guy, who told me he was born in 1970. That was a discrepancy I just couldn't blame on inexact carbon dating."

Breakey then embarked on an

investigation of Tuttle, turning up a long history of chicanery. During an eclectic career that has spanned decades, Tuttle has variously claimed to have found Wilbur Wright's first paper airplane, a signed author's copy of Homer's *The Odyssey* and the original recipe for shepherd's pie. All of these discoveries were in time proven false.

His most unusual hoax, though, occurred more than four decades ago. Tuttle, who earned his M.D. from Berlinische Polytechnic in Germany, staged his own death during the Korean War after a brief stint in a U.S. Mobile Army Surgical Hospital. Details are unclear, but Tuttle was alleged to have died after jumping from a chopper without a parachute. "About that, I can only confirm that I'm no longer dead," Tuttle wrote in an e-mailed response to an interview request.

Officials at Egan Academy said they had no plans to rescind Tuttle's job offer. "He brings an awful lot to the table in terms of Texas history," explained headmaster Max Patchogue. "Did you know he has the only reel-to-reel recording of Davy Crockett's Alamo speech?" ●

CUSTOM MADE

Where li'l dogies of wonder are roped and tied with the lasso of revelation.

Why do baseball managers wear uniforms?

Terry Francona, manager, Philadelphia Phillies: I don't know, but I'm sure glad we do. **Why's that?** Frankly, I'm a terrible dresser, and I look better in a hat. **You do wear it well.** I wonder why coaches in other sports don't wear uniforms. Look at Joe Paterno. He wears nice pants, but they're all rolled up. **That's a good look.** *Stefano Tonchi, creative fashion director, Esquire:* One of the worst things a man can do is not dress for his age. But the manager of a team has to be comfortable, and move freely on the field. **So true.** But no stripes! Stripes are not so good on people who are not skinny. It is not pleasurable for the eyes. **Amen.** *Frank Vito, researcher, Baseball Hall of Fame:* It dates back to when teams had player-managers. They needed to be in uniform. **Who says?** It's a rule. Anyone on the field is required to be in uniform. **What about trainers?** Hmmm ... that's true. **Ha!** Well, baseball is the oldest professional sport, so maybe we should ask why coaches of other sports don't wear uniforms. **Maybe we should leave the questions to me—Answer Guy.** You know, one of the only exceptions to managers wearing uniforms was Connie Mack. He wore a suit. But he wasn't allowed on the field. [*Ed.'s*

note: *Mack sent his pitching coach instead.*] **Guess we should call Connie then.** *Spokesperson, Senator Connie Mack (R-Fla.):* Wrong Connie Mack. The senator is his grandson, and he's busy. **Can you ask the senator about the suit anyway?** [*Two days later ...*] He was a gentleman on and off the field, and dressed the part. **Well, not *on* the field.**

Where the dinghies of quizzicality are anchored to the mooring post of indubitability.

Why do baseball players throw it around the horn?

Darrin Fletcher, catcher, Toronto Blue Jays: Tradition. **Fascinating.** *Jason Varitek, catcher, Boston Red Sox:* I'd have to say it's tradition. **Have to or want to?** *Eric Enders, researcher, Baseball Hall of Fame:* It's tradi... **Got ya. Any idea why it's tradi...?** Guess they've got nothing better to do. **Clearly.** It goes back at least to 1912. When they'd put a new ball in play, they'd toss it around the infield, and the players would scuff it up and spit on it and stuff. Gave the pitcher an advantage. **Cheaters.** *Red Foley, official scorer, New York Yankees:* It goes way back. **So I'm told.** Before they had canals, they went "around the Horn" to get to San Francisco. It took, like, eight months. **You lost me, Red.** You know, whadayacallit, Cape Horn, down there on the bottom of South America. **They used to throw the ball around South America?** No, no, no. The boats. **What boats?** The steamer ships or what have you. Before they built the Panama Canal [*Ed.'s note: 1914.*], they had to go all the way around Cape Horn. That's where the term comes from. **But what does throwing the ball around the infield have to do with old-time navigation routes?** *Paul Dickson, author, The New Dickson*

South America
Dates of Independence from 1811-1830

Guyana 1966
Surinam 1975
French Guiana

Venezuela 1830
Colombia 1819
Ecuador 1822
Peru 1824
Bolivia 1825
Brazilian Empire 1822
Paraguay 1811
Argentina 1816
Uruguay 1828
Chile 1818

FORMER SPANISH TERRITORY 1812
BOUNDARIES AT INDEPENDENCE

Baseball Dictionary: Baseball's full of nautical terms: "around the horn," "on deck," "in the hole," "skipper." **Aye.** Back in the day, we were a seafaring nation. Over time, the language of the sea came ashore. **Time and tide wait for no man.** Exactly. We know that "on deck" and "in the hole" came out of Belfast, Maine, in 1872. The Red Sox were barnstorming, and the local scorekeeper announced, "Moody at bat, Boardman on deck, Dinsmore in the hold." Boston's scorekeeper thought it was cool and brought it to the big leagues. Over time, "hold" became "hole." **Yar, dude.**

Where the conniving hands of flimflammery are shackled by a straight-shooting lawman.

Why do baseball fans stretch in the seventh inning?

Shane Spencer, outfielder, New York Yankees: I bet people want to get one more beer before the vendors close. **Could be.** *Frank Vito, researcher, Baseball Hall of Fame:* In 1910, President Taft stood up in the seventh inning on Opening Day between the A's and the Senators. Everybody else got up out of respect. **Respect for what?** The president. **How quaint.** But an earlier story credits Brother Jasper of Manhattan College. *Bill Buran, sports information assistant, Manhattan College:* Brother Jasper was the baseball coach, but he was also the Prefect of Discipline. It was very strict back then. The students had to sit still. No slouching. **That *is* strict.** In 1882, we played the New York Metropolitans. It was hot and sticky. When we came to bat in the seventh, Brother Jasper told the students they could move about and stretch their legs. **But how did it spread?** We played the Giants every year at the Polo Grounds. Giant fans saw the students stretch, so they did, too. It caught on from there. **What about Taft?** *Ray Henderson, chief of interpretations, William Howard Taft National Historic Site:* Lore says he stood up and fans thought he was leaving, so they stood up, too.

But, you know, he was from Cincinnati, and it really started here in Cincinnati. **Hmmm. Wonder if the Hall knows about this.** *Vito:* Now that you mention it, Harry Wright of the Red Stockings did write a letter in 1869 that tells of Cincy fans standing up in the seventh. **Why?** [*Reads*] "To enjoy the relief afforded by relaxation from a long posture upon hard benches." **And to get one more beer?** Could be.

Where the class-cutting slacker of doltishness is busted by the eraser-clapping hall monitor of acuity.

Why do they use Xs and Os in football diagrams?

Pete Fierle, information services manager, Pro Football Hall of Fame: It's hard to say when it started. We have playbooks from the '20s that use Xs and Os. **Oh, really.** O indicates the offense. But D is too similar to O, so for defense, they used an X. **Ah.** *Alan Grant, ex-NFLer and Answer Guy colleague at ESPN The Magazine:* Actually, they don't really use Xs and Os anymore. **Oh, no?** No. They use all kinds of different symbols: letters, numbers, even squares and triangles. **How exciting!** By the way, why are you calling me? You're two desks away. **Al, you know better than to question Answer Guy.** *Ron Jaworski, ex-NFLer and Answer Guy colleague at ESPN the network:* The symbols vary from team to team. They use specific letters to indicate specific positions, like T for tackle, S for safety. **Pretty exacting.** Some teams have nicknames for each position. Like the weakside safety is often called Jill, so he gets a J. **Jill?** I guess it's an allusion to the female being weaker. **Sexists!** *Jay Paterno, assistant football coach, Penn State:* We still use O for offense, because those positions don't really change from play to play. I mean, a guard's a guard, a tackle's a tackle. **Obviously.**

But defenses are so complex that an X isn't sufficient. You have to know who that X is. **To eliminate the X-factor?** Kinda. It's like shorthand. **How so?** Instead of saying strongside linebacker all the time, we call him Sam. He gets a dollar sign. **Why?** Because S is taken. For the safety. **Clever.** When we watch game film, it's like we're speaking in code: "They've got a great Sam" or "Where was Fritz on that play?" **Fritz?** That's the weakside linebacker. He gets an F. **Who's Fritz?** Fritz DeFluri. He was a pizza guy around here in the '60s. **Good thing his name wasn't Otto.** Exactly.

Where the shadow of doubt is dissipated by the penetrating lamp of knowledge.

Why do officials wear black-and-white stripes?

Juanita Campbell, National Football Officials Alliance: I'm sure it's some kind of tradition. But ask my husband, Jim. **Okay. Jim, your wife said you'd know why officials wear black and white.** *Jim Campbell, coordinator of football officials, Conference USA:* Yes, ma'am. **Ma'am?** I mean sir. When I hear "wife" I automatically say, "Yes, ma'am." **That's nice, Jim.** Anyway, it's tradition. **So I'm told.** I can tell you why goalposts used to be 20 feet, 7 inches. **Please do.** That was the longest two-by-four they made back then. [*Ed.'s note: Campbell's no goalpost expert; they were never that size.*] **Now, about those refs?** It's like Exxon. **It is?** Yes. Industrialist Raymond Lloyd chose "Exxon" because it meant nothing in any language. [*Ed.: Campbell's no Exxon expert, either; the company has never heard of Lloyd.*] It just is what it is. Black and white works. **Works how?** *Barrie Frost, professor of psychology, Queen's University at Kingston, Canada:* It's a matter of carving out chunks of perceptual space that are maximally different from any team's uniform. **Uh-huh. But why stripes? Why not, say, polka dots?** *Donald Teig, optometrist:*

Stripes are more stimulating to the retina than polka dots. **Wow. So who was the genius who figured this out?** *Joe Horrigan, vice president of communications, Pro Football Hall of Fame:* The modern ref jersey was first used at Eastern Michigan University, in Ypsilanti. *Mike Bond, sports historian, Eastern Michigan University:* Lloyd Olds, our track coach, came up with it. He also refereed football and basketball, and he got tired of players throwing him the ball all the time. In 1914 he had a relative knit him a black and white shirt. **Decided to carve out a chunk of the ol' perceptual space, eh?** I think it was more so he wouldn't get hit.

Where uncertainty, like a flushed duck, is dropped from the sky with a truth-finding shotgun. In-season only.

Why are blue lines solid and red lines checkered?

Red Fisher, longtime hockey writer, Montreal: I have no idea. I've never heard that question in my life. *David Baker, NHL officiating department:* The NHL rule book says: "With reference to the center red line, this line shall contain regular interval markings of a uniform, distinctive design, which will readily distinguish it from the two blue lines." **Yeah, but why?** I'm not sure. *Tracey Green, intern, Hockey Hall of Fame:* It's because of TV, to distinguish the red line from the blue lines on a black-and-white TV. **You sure?** Well, we have no proof. There's nothing in the rule book about that. **When was the broken red line established?** For the 1951–52 season. **But wait—did they even broadcast hockey in the early '50s?** I'm not sure. **For them to change the rule for TV, hockey must have been huge back then.** Uh, it could've been. *Dan Diamond, editor, Total Hockey:* 1964 was the year the checkered line was made official. **They had to use a checkered line?** Well, some use a checkered line, some use three parallel lines—the rule can be interpreted a number of ways. **So as long as the line's broken up somehow, you can put in pictures of, say, Elmo?** *Baker:*

Well, actually you're not supposed
to have logos interrupt the line.
The Hamilton Bulldogs have a huge
bulldog logo in the middle of the
ice—the refs can't read the line at
all. **Well, that's Hamilton for you—
they always have to do things their
own way.** I won't comment on that.

Where ushers of erudition escort you to seats of learning.

Why do we sit in the stands?

Carrie Plummer, publicity director, HOK Sport: When we design stadia, we don't call them "stands," we call them "seating bowls." **Subtly evasive.** I have a theory, though. **Love those.** Maybe it comes from "grandstanding." When a guy makes an easy play look hard, he's showing off for the fans in the stands. **That sounds pretty chicken, Carrie. I'm an egg man.** *John Thorn, coeditor, Total Baseball:* It's short for "grandstand." **Lucky lady! But shouldn't it be grandsit?** *Steve Perrault, director of defining, Merriam-Webster, Inc.:* No, no. The stands themselves are standing, like a hot dog stand, or a newsstand. **Extra! Extra!** *Ronald Smith, secretary treasurer, North American Society for Sport History:* In the early days of sports, mainly horse racing, the upper class sat in carriages around the track. **O most noble steed, gallop hastily!** Commoners stood or maybe climbed trees. **Move yer bloomin' arse!** *Allen Guttman, author, Sports Spectators:* Grandstands have been around for thousands of years. They're meant to provide a better view. **Adside in anticum!** [Ed.'s note: Down in front!] They also segregated patrons by social class, which, until fairly recently, was based on birth status, not wealth. **How gauche.** *Paul*

Dickson, author, The New Dickson Baseball Dictionary: The geography of early baseball stadiums was very much based on the movement of the sun. The more expensive seats were in the shade, while the cheapest ones were exposed to direct sunlight. They called them "bleachers," from bleaching boards, a jocular reference to fans being bleached like sheets drying in the sun. **Have to take your word for it. I send my laundry out.**

Where unschooled insects are zapped by the bug light of pedagogy.

Why do track and field go together?

Tom, PR department, U.S. Track & Field Association: Beats me. I don't even know why peanut butter and jelly go together, and I've been eating it for 42 years. **Oo-kay then.** *Dan O'Brien, Olympic decathlete, USA:* Traditionally, all the events—running, throwing, jumping—were activities of war. **Really?** Look at the marathon. It's based on the guy at the battle of Marathon who ran to Athens and announced the victory. [*Ed.'s note: Greeks over Persians, 490 B.C.*] Then he dropped dead from exhaustion. **Good ol' Philippides.** *Dave Johnson, director, Penn Relays:* The 16-pound shot weighs the same as a British cannonball. **You don't say?** And the Greeks flung the discus at enemies. **Hmmm.** In the javelin, they measure distance, not accuracy, which shows it's a war thing, not a hunting thing. **Interesting.** The pole vault was used for assaults on fortifications. **Attack!** The sack race and three-legged race used to be events, too. **War *is* hell.** *Jerry Quiller, track coach, U.S. Military Academy:* Patton was an Olympian. Modern pentathlon: fencing, running, shooting, swimming, and equestrian. **All at once?** No. *Phew.* Anyway, it probably goes back to the Greeks. **What does?** Track and field. The guys not eaten by lions had to run around

until they dropped dead. **Sounds Roman to me.** Whatever. By the way, it's called athletics everywhere else in the world. **What is?** Track and field. But Americans didn't know what the hell "athletics" meant. Like that metric stuff. *Yeesh. Giorgio Reineri, media relations director, International Amateur Athletic Federation, Monaco:* Many of these things are helpful in battle. Before the horse, you had to run to war. **Or from it.** True. But really, to run and to jump and to throw are natural expressions of what humans do on the earth. **Beautiful.** In the sea? Different story.

Marching the army of elucidation over the Alps of befuddlement.

Why is the A's mascot an elephant?

Debbie Gallas, public relations assistant, Oakland A's: "Stomper" is very popular. **That's nice.** Sometimes he brings his wife to the games. **He's married?** Well, she might be his girlfriend. **How can you tell?** I could ask him. **You speak elephant?** No, no. Stomper's not an elephant. He's a guy in an elephant suit. *Sure he is.* Anyway, it goes back to Connie Mack, when the A's were in Philadelphia. **Ah, yes, pachyderm country.** Before the 1902 season, Giants manager John McGraw dismissed the new A's as a bunch of "white elephants." **Meaning?** You know, like a white-elephant sale. **Actually, I was hoping you knew.** *Alan Dundes, professor of anthropology and folklore, UC Berkeley:* "White elephant" refers to a burdensome gift or purchase that's too valuable to throw away. It may come from Thailand, where albino elephants are sacred. Legend says that when the king was displeased with a subject, he would give him a white elephant, knowing the cost of keeping it would cause his ruination. **It's good to be the king.** *John O'Donnell, volunteer, Philadelphia A's Historical Society:* McGraw's comment was derogatory, implying that the A's were worthless. But Mack made it a positive thing. **That's *so* Led**

Zeppelin. It's been part of A's folklore ever since, sort of a good-luck charm. **Elephants are lucky?** *Receptionist, Bronx Zoo:* Our mammal department takes calls from three to four only. **Do they get many calls?** No. **Odd.** *Norm B., spiritualist, Amherst, Mass.:* The elephant is a good-luck beast. **Why?** For one, in prehistoric times, one mastodon could feed a lot of people. Second, the meat contained L-tryptophan, a mild hallucinogen. **Magically delicious!**

Where the diapers of exasperation are changed by the steady-handed father of contentment.

Why are so many car races 500 miles long?

Mark Lewis, communications coordinator, Daytona Motor Speedway: Here's the deal. **Dish it.** Daytona founder Bill France, Sr., decided he wanted them to race 500 miles. **Why?** Well, 500 is the American standard for a featured race event. **Yes, I know, but could you tell me why?** If you're asking me how Mr. France settled on that number, I don't think anyone can say. **Why not?** Because they'd have to pick a dead man's brain. **Yipe!** *Buz McKim, NASCAR archivist:* I think it's more tradition than anything else. **Since when?** In the early '50s, there were only two 500-mile races, Indy and Charlotte. Most races were more like a hundred. **Piece of cake.** Not really. The tracks were dirt. The cars couldn't make it much farther. **God bless blacktop.** Indeed. And, as the cars got faster, the races got too quick. Five hundred miles gave fans their money's worth. *Donald Davidson, historian, Indianapolis Motor Speedway:* The Speedway was originally built [*Ed.'s note: 1909.*] as a testing facility for new cars. But Carl Fisher [*Ed.: The track's cofounder.*] realized that quality entertainment could help increase sales of cars. **Dogs and ponies?** Exactly. In '10, they had three short races, but

attendance was lousy. In '11, they launched the 500. It was a huge success. **Yeah, yeah, that's nice. But why the Indy *500*? Why not the Indy 600, or the Indy 487?** Well, they wanted a race that would last all day, like eight hours. [*Ed.: The first race was 6:42.*] Two hundred laps on a 2.5-mile track gives you 500 miles. It just seemed right. **Pretty lame answer.** Sometimes answers aren't what we want them to be. **You're preachin' to the choir there, Don. Now, about Jim Nabors ...** Oh, he's very popular here. **Is there anyone, anywhere who can tell me why?** Now *that's* a good question. **Shazam!**

Where the roll call of inquiry is
answered with a resounding "Here!"

Why are there five
Olympic rings?

*Anne Marie Cruz, Olympics reporter,
ESPN The Magazine:* Oh, no! **What's
wrong?** If I don't come up with
something interesting, I'll feel bad.
The truth will set you free. Maybe it
has something to do with the colors
of the rainbow. **There's no black in a
rainbow.** Black's not a color. **But it
is an Olympic ring.** Hmmm. Maybe it
has to do with weather: yellow for
sunshine, blue for water, green for
trees, red for blood. **Bloody weather?**
Could be. **Maybe I should ask your
boss.** *Sue Hovey, Olympics editor, ESPN
The Magazine:* I have absolutely no
idea. **Pity.** Wait, don't print that!
Okay. Hold on—each ring represents
a continent. **There are only five
rings.** So? **Have you counted the
continents lately?** Antarctica doesn't
count. **Why not?** Nobody lives there.
*Mary Johnson, Antarctic Support
Associates:* There are more than 1,000
people living in Antarctica. **Then why
don't they get an Olympic ring?** I
don't know how to respond to that.
Chris Weston, PR specialist, USOC:
There's not much to the rings. **No
kidding.** The five rings represent the
five original continents. *Hovey:* Ha!
There were only five? *Dr. Ramon
Arrowsmith, geologist, Arizona State
University:* Actually, there was only
one. Pangaea. **And how many are**

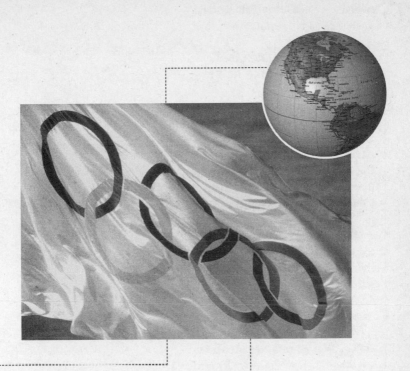

there now? Hard to say. A continent is a large land mass made up of granitic crustal material. **Obviously.** So India, Arabia, Madagascar, even New Guinea could all be considered continents. **But they don't have Olympic rings. How sad.** *David Wallechinsky, Olympics historian:* IOC founder Pierre de Coubertin came up with the rings around 1914. He counted North and South America as one continent. **Moron.** The interlocking rings represent the unity of all nations. **That's beautiful.** De Coubertin's heart is buried in Olympia. **Where's the rest of him?** No clue.

Nourishing the buds of truth with the cooling rains of scholarship.

Why do college basketball champs cut down the nets?

Tracy Dittemore, NCAA Hall of Champions: I'm the historian here, and I have no idea. Maybe Bill Hancock will know. Do you know Bill? **Uh, no.** Well, he's not here, anyway. **Bummer.** *Allen Barra, sports historian:* I think it started in Kentucky. Their football team never used to win anything, so they couldn't tear down the goalposts. By the way, when you think about it, cutting the nets is an inexpensive way to celebrate. And it doesn't destroy property. **True.** *Billy Packer, college basketball analyst, CBS Sports:* Everett Case, coach at N.C. State. It started with him. **Cool. Do you know ...** [*click!*] *Skeeter Francis, former sports information director, ACC:* ... **how he came up with it?** As I remember, it started when Everett came to State in the late '40s. They won the Southern Conference championship and cut down the net. **Yeah, but do you have any idea why?** Not really. Maybe he brought it with him from Indiana. *Jeremiah Johnson, intern, Indiana Basketball Hall of Fame:* [*Rustle of newspapers*] Looks like Case was the guy, but there's no word here on how it got started. I did find someone for you who played for Case when he coached at Frankfort (Ind.) High School. *Evan "Red" Thompson, former*

forward, Frankfort High Hot Dogs· Now, I'm 89 years old, so you'll have to bear with me. **Yes, sir.** We went to the finals in '29 and '30. We won it in '29, and I'm pretty sure we cut down the nets. But it seemed like that's what we were supposed to do, like it was already a tradition. Whether Case came up with it, I can't say. **Hey, Jeremiah, this thing's older than Red. Got anything else?** *Johnson:* Well, net cutting has always been a big deal in Indiana. My team never made it past the sectionals, but ... **All right, then ...** By the way, I applied for an internship at ESPN. I was wondering ... **Say no more. I'll put in a good word for you.**

Faithfully executing the office of inquisitiveness.

Why does the president phone the Super Bowl winner?

Frank Ceresi, curator, MCI National Sports Gallery: It started in the early '70s, and it's been a tradition ever since. But presidents have always maintained a keen interest in sports. **Bread and circuses?** Perhaps. Ulysses S. Grant had an audience with the undefeated Cincinnati Red Stockings in 1869. **Bottoms up!** And Teddy Roosevelt pretty much saved football. **Way ahead of ya.** [*Ed.'s note: See page 10.*] Even George Washington played ball with his troops at Valley Forge. **Bet they let him win.** *Saleem Choudhry, researcher, Pro Football Hall of Fame:* Nixon was the first to phone the winners' locker room. He called the Chiefs after Super Bowl IV. **Any idea why?** No. He had a six-minute chat with MVP Len Dawson. **About?** He told him the world looks up to pro football players. **Yeah, they're batty for them in Botswana.** He also called Redskins coach George Allen before a playoff game in '71 and suggested a play. **Secret bombing campaign?** Flanker reverse. **Tricky.** *Susan Naulty, archivist, Richard Nixon Library and Birthplace:* On Jan. 11, 1970, the president spoke long distance with Chiefs coach Hank Stram, from 3:19 to 3:20. **Before the game?** Apparently. **So the fix *was* in.** We don't know what was said. The taping

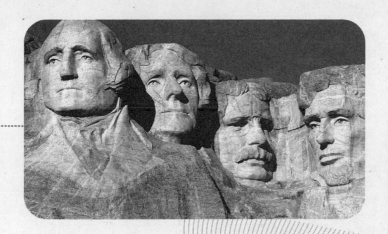

system wasn't in place yet. **Expletive deleted!** Nixon loved sports, and was influenced by Wallace Newman, his football coach at Whittier College. **Go Poets!** He didn't play much, and only got in when there was no hope of winning or no chance to lose. **How apt.** But he learned the values of sportsmanship and fair play, and practiced them all his life. **Oh, Susan, you must be new there.**

Where the broth of banality is complexified by the naturally occurring spices of intricacy.

Why don't they allow pepper at major league ballparks?

May, at the American Spice Trade Association: I'm not sure that we are the right people to help you. **Why not? Pepper's a spice, isn't it?** Well, yes it is. **So then?** They're talking about the game pepper. **Oh. Right. Of course they are.** Perhaps you should try ... **Why do they call it pepper, anyway?** I really don't know. **Could you guess?** Well, it is a warmup game, right? **Allegedly.** Maybe they want to fire people up before the game. You know, because pepper is on the hot side. **'Tis.** *Bill Francis, researcher, Baseball Hall of Fame:* George Wright of the original Cincinnati Red Stockings [*Ed.'s note: 1869–70.*] is credited with starting the first pepper game. **Good ol' George.** Players stood in a semicircle and pitched the ball at short range to a batter who would "pepper" it back. It was billed as a juggling act, a real crowd pleaser. It was banned around the 1950s. *A Yankee Stadium spokesman:* It's more discouraged than banned. **That's not what the signs say.** We took our signs down. Players should know by now. **Okay, so why is it discouraged?** *Jorge Posada, catcher, New York Yankees:* They don't want people getting hurt. **What people?** People in the stands, I guess. **Wimps.**

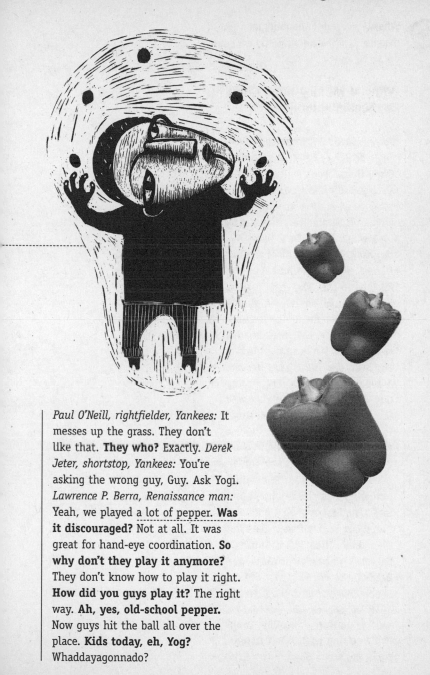

Paul O'Neill, rightfielder, Yankees: It messes up the grass. They don't like that. **They who?** Exactly. *Derek Jeter, shortstop, Yankees:* You're asking the wrong guy, Guy. Ask Yogi. *Lawrence P. Berra, Renaissance man:* Yeah, we played a lot of pepper. **Was it discouraged?** Not at all. It was great for hand-eye coordination. **So why don't they play it anymore?** They don't know how to play it right. **How did you guys play it?** The right way. **Ah, yes, old-school pepper.** Now guys hit the ball all over the place. **Kids today, eh, Yog?** Whaddayagonnado?

Where the gnats of incompetence are hit with the rolled-up newspaper of know-how.

Why do we sing the national anthem at sporting events?

Saleem Choudhry, researcher, Pro Football Hall of Fame: Don't know. **Okay then.** *Seana Jones, intern, Hockey Hall of Fame:* The NHL established in 1946 that the anthem be played before every game. **Any idea why?** Not really. *Donald Davidson, historian, Indianapolis Motor Speedway:* No idea, but in England in the '30s, they played "God Save the King" at the end of movies and plays. People ran for the exits to beat the song, otherwise they had to stand and listen until it was over. The heathens. *Bill Francis, researcher, Baseball Hall of Fame:* Is this Answer Guy? **Uh, maybe.** We *love* Answer Guy. **Oh, yeah, it's Answer Guy.** It started in World War I. The Cubs were playing the Red Sox in the World Series. **Ha!** Patriotic fervor was rampant, and during the seventh-inning stretch, the band just broke into "The Star-Spangled Banner." Everybody took off their hats and sang along. **Nice.** But it didn't become tradition until World War II. **Patriotic fervor?** Exactly. *Nina Gilbert, director of choral activities, Lafayette College:* The original tune was an old British drinking song, "To Anacreon in Heav'n." **Catchy.** Anacreon was a Greek poet [*Ed.'s note:*

563–478 B.C.] who wrote about love and wine. **'Atta boy.** The song was still popular in 1812 when Francis Scott Key wrote new words. He was a hymn writer, and that's what they did—write new words for old songs. **Interesting.** What's really interesting is that he was kind of sticking it to the British. **Do tell.** Those bombs were designed to burst on target, not in the air. And the rockets didn't do damage, they just lit up the sky. That's why he could see the flag waving in the first place. **Hey, yeah!** It's got an "in your face" quality that most people miss. **Not anymore, sister. Not anymore.**

TIME-OUT ⊙ The Answer Guy Quiz*

You've read the book, now see if you remember any of it.

1. **How many legal ways are there to get to first base?**
   - Ⓐ 23
   - Ⓑ 43
   - Ⓒ 63
   - Ⓓ A lot less than the Hall of Fame guy says if you don't count all the repeats and technicalities

2. **What is the origin of "deuce" in tennis?**
   - Ⓐ It's from the Spanish for "tie"
   - Ⓑ It's from the French for "tie"
   - Ⓒ It's from the French for "two to win"
   - Ⓓ It's from the French for "Manfred Mann's version is better than Springsteen's"

3. **What was the Kentucky Derby almost called?**
   - Ⓐ The Kentucky Fried Derby
   - Ⓑ The Kentucky Top Hat
   - Ⓒ The Kentucky Bunbury
   - Ⓓ The National Endowment for the Arts

4. **Who was captain of the Hamm's bowling team in the 1930s?**
   - Ⓐ James T. Kirk
   - Ⓑ Rags Ragogna
   - Ⓒ Carmine Ragusa
   - Ⓓ Mia Hamm

5. **What was early baseball originally intended to provoke?**
   - Ⓐ Fights
   - Ⓑ Frankincense
   - Ⓒ Mirth
   - Ⓓ Collective bargaining

6. When was Answer Guy born?
- Ⓐ 6/1/70
- Ⓑ 1294 B.C.
- Ⓒ February 9, 1964
- Ⓓ Yesterday

7. What does the CCM on hockey equipment stand for?
- Ⓐ Canadian Car Mechanics
- Ⓑ Canadian Cycle and Motor Company
- Ⓒ Canadian Crease Minders
- Ⓓ Choosy Moms Choose Jif (They dropped the "J" in '56)

8. Frederick, the original dark horse, was said to have ...?
- Ⓐ Shed an unpleasant and irksome light upon the visual orbs of the knowing ones
- Ⓑ Shed lots of hair upon the newly upholstered love seats of the smarmy ones
- Ⓒ Been a misunderstood genius of a horse who was constantly picked on because he wore glasses and played violin
- Ⓓ Pretty well sucked, as dark horses are wont to

9. What do they call a mulligan in Ireland?
- Ⓐ A correction shot
- Ⓑ A Schwartz
- Ⓒ A Paddy O'Furniture
- Ⓓ Cheating

10. What is Answer Guy's preferred means of ablution?
- Ⓐ The shower
- Ⓑ The tub
- Ⓒ A splash of water and some deodorant
- Ⓓ Two Hail Marys and an Our Father

---

*USE NO. 2 (OR 3) PENCIL

◯ ⬤ ◯ ◯

11. Why couldn't Lord Horatio Nelson do a full nelson, even if he wanted to?

(A) He was a Mormon

(B) He only had one arm

(C) He was a lover, not a fighter

(D) He had already paid other people to do it for him

12. What did the Greek poet Anacreon write about?

(A) Sex and drugs

(B) Flags

(C) Love and wine

(D) Archery

13. Which of the following can be said of Fritz DeFluri?

(A) He delivered pizza

(B) His name is not Otto

(C) Nittany Lions coaches named their weakside linebacker after him

(D) All of the above

14. Answer Guy is

(A) A leg man

(B) An egg man

(C) The walrus

(D) Ringo

15. Why don't people like fractions?

(A) Fractions don't like people

(B) They're unwieldy

(C) Fractions are divisive

(D) People are idiots

ANSWERS: 1. A (D is also acceptable); 2. C; 3. C; 4. B; 5. C; 6. A; 7. B; 8. A; 9. D; 10. B; 11. B; 12. C; 13. D; 14. B; 15. B

KEY: 0–4, Answer Pup; 5–8, Answer Lad; 9–11, Answer Stud; 11–15, Paying way too much attention—now go outside and play!

INDEX ⊙

A

A Midsummer Night's Dream, **90**
archery, **84–85**, **112**

B

baseball
    base running counterclockwise,
      20–21
    Boston Red Sox, **102–103**
    bullpen, **110–111**
    Cartwright, Alexander, **24–25**
    Coriolis effect, **21**
    home plate, **76–77**
    manager's uniforms, **126–127**
    number of innings, **24–25**
    numerology in, **25**
    pepper in, **152–153**
    pitching mound, **28–29**
    seventh inning stretch, **130–131**
    stealing first base, **30–31**
    strikeouts, **82–83**
    throw it around the horn,
      128–129
    uniform pant stirrups, **58–59**
    Wadsworth, Lewis F., **24**
    World Series, **78–79**
basketball
    basket point value, **8–9**
    cagers, **94–95**
    college, **148–149**
    cutting down nets, **148–149**
    foul shot, **9**
    shot clock, **18–19**
    "top of the key," **94–95**
bicycle racing, **38–39**
birdies, **112–113**
bogey, **112–113**
Boston Red Sox, **102–103**
bowling
    300-point game, **22–23**
    kegels, **23**
    Saint Boniface, **23**
    shoes, **46–47**

strikes and spares, **114–115**
boxing ring, **40–41**
Brown, Paul, **52–53**
bullpen, **110–111**
bull's-eye, **84–85**

C

cagers, **94–95**
calling "fore," **86–87**
calling "hike," **88–89**
Camp, Walter, **88–89**
Canadian Football League, **12**
car racing
    and bicycle racing, **38–39**
    checkered signal flag, **38–39**
    pit stops, **80–81**
    race lengths, **144–145**
Cartwright, Alexander, **24–25**
chains, for marking yards in football,
    42–43
Champion, Albert, **39**
charley horse, **104–105**
Chevrolet, Louie, **39**
Chrysler, Walter, **39**
Cleveland Browns, **52–53**
college basketball, **148–149**
college football, **54–55**, **60–61**
Coriolis effect, **21**
counterclockwise base running,
    20–21
cricket, **74–75**, **92–93**
cutting down nets in basketball,
    148–149

D

dark horse, **106–107**
de Coubertin, Pierre, **147**

E

Earl of Derby, **16–17**
eighteen holes in golf, **14–15**

N

names of sports
  ice hockey, **70–71**
  soccer, **72–73**
naming of sports
  cricket, **74–75**
national anthem, **154–155**
nelsons, **116–117**
nets in basketball, **148–149**
Nixon, President Richard, **150–151**
numerology and baseball, **25**

O

Oakland A's, **142–143**
officials and referees, **134–135**
Olympic rings, **146–147**

P

pepper in baseball, **152–153**
pit stops, **80–81**
pitchers, **110–111**
pitching mound, **28–29**
Pittsburgh Steelers, **50–51**
play area lines, **136–137**
play diagrams, **132–133**
point values in basketball, **8–9**
Presidents of the United States,
  10, 150–151
pucks, **90–91**
purse, **11**

Q

quarterbacks, **96–97**

R

race lengths, **144–145**
Roosevelt, Teddy, **150–151**
  football, **10–11**
round of golf, **14–15**
rounders, **20–21**
rugby, **12–13, 97**

S

safety equipment
  golf, **86–87**
  ice hockey, **44–45**
Saint Boniface, **23**
sand traps, **56–57**
scoring systems
  archery, **84–85**
  baseball, **82–83**
  bowling, **114–115**
  golf, **112–113**
  ice hockey, **92–93**
  tennis, **26–27**
seventh inning stretch, **130–131**
shoes, bowling, **46–47**
shot clock in basketball, **18–19**
soccer
  naming of, **72–73**
special teams, **97–99**
sports etymology
  Boston Red Sox, **102–103**
  Toronto Maple Leafs, **100–101**
St. Andrew's, Scotland, **14**
stakes, **41**
stands, **138–139**
stealing first base, **30–31**
strikeouts, **82–83**
strikes and spares, **114–115**
Super Bowl, **150–151**
sweating, **62–63**
swimming, **62–63**

T

tennis
  balls, **48–49**
  scoring system, **26–27**
The Star-Spangled Banner,
  154–155
three-hundred-point bowling game,
  22–23
three-year-olds in Kentucky Derby,
  16–17
throw it around the horn, **128–129**
"top of the key," **94–95**
Toronto Maple Leafs, **100–101**
track and field, **140–141**